W9-AWT-462

6/5

MY
APPOINTED
ROUND

MY APPOINTED ROUND

HOLT,
RINEHART
AND WINSTON

929
DAYS AS
POSTMASTER
GENERAL

BY
J. EDWARD DAY

NEW YORK
CHICAGO
SAN FRANCISCO

Designer: Ernst Reichl
81770-0115
Printed in the United States of America

Dedicated

to

Mary Louise

TABLE OF CONTENTS

1 The Least Known   1

2 Pull Helps   7

3 Fowl Play   15

4 The Rumor Maneuver   24

5 Lady Chatterley's *What?*   29

6 From A(BCD) to Z(IP)   38

7 No Business Like P.O. Business   47

8 Man's Best Friend Has Teeth   60

9 The Party Faithful   70

10 "He's a Democrat"   83

11 The View from the Limousine Window   95

12 Talking Turkey   113

13 Orientation Course for Innocents   124

14 The Prosperity President   135

15 All the Way with LBJ   142

Chapter 1
THE LEAST
KNOWN

WHEN the original Kennedy Cabinet was appointed, some wag dubbed it "nine unknowns and one brother."

I was the least known of all. So unknown, in fact, that in the first weeks after my arrival in Washington the Speaker of the House, Sam Rayburn, mistook me for a bouncer and ordered me to clear away a crowd of gawkers waiting around a doorway for the President.

At another gathering, when introduced as the Postmaster General, I was asked politely, "postmaster of *where?*" And as plain Mr. Day I grew accustomed at parties to receiving looks that weren't so much at me as beyond me to the crowded room where, presumably, those of *real* importance waited.

In the confusion caused by the advent of the New Frontier's new faces on the Washington scene, it was of course understandable that I was not immediately recognized by the natives.

What really did surprise me, however, was when I began to have difficulty recognizing myself. In the press I was headlined as a law partner of Adlai Stevenson, although I had been only a law clerk in the huge Chicago firm of which he was a partner. I was described as a successful novelist, although my one effort, written many years before, amassed me something less than a fortune in royalties—the last payment being 40 cents in postage stamps. Suddenly I was a daring war hero, even though my four years in the Navy consisted of uneventful convoy duty. And I, who can barely stay afloat in an inner tube, was billed as an ardent swimmer. The secret life of Walter Mitty had suddenly become public.

Indeed, in trying to make an athlete of me to fit the image of the New Frontier, *Sports Illustrated* magazine, rejecting my offer to pose with the power lawn mower (not vigorous enough, they said), photographed me in a smashing serve on a neighbor's tennis court. On examination, however, the picture showed a great many dry leaves scattered about the court, giving it a definitely unused look. What the picture didn't reveal was worse: the tennis racket was my daughter's. I had had to borrow it for the occasion.

Except for my lack of prowess at touch football (or, generally, any athletic activity more strenuous than croquet), I had the qualifications for a post in the Kennedy Administration: I went to Harvard; I served in the Navy; my wife went to Vassar; and I had been associated with Adlai Stevenson. In addition, the bishop of our Methodist district in Southern California was named Kennedy, making me one of the original Methodists for Kennedy.

But as to the real reasons why I was chosen, I was as mystified as anybody.

Until January 20, 1961, I was a senior vice president of Prudential Insurance Company, in charge of one and a half billion dollars in investments and 7,500 employees in thirteen Western states.

After January 20, I was the least-known Cabinet member and no one, including myself, understood how I got there. It was particularly surprising that I would be appointed Postmaster General, a highly political post.

I had met the President-elect only a few times; our acquaintance was very slight. I had not been active in the 1960 Presidential campaign. I had even declined to serve as Los Angeles area chairman of Citizens for Kennedy because I was busy as treasurer and chief strategist of a nonpartisan state bond issue to bring water from Northern California to the parched south.

I had never run for elective office. My only previous experience in government had been as a reform insurance commissioner in Adlai Stevenson's administration when he was Governor of Illinois. In a published article I had opposed medical care for the aged under Social Security. And, contrary to rumor, I was never a significant contributor or fund-raiser for the Democratic Party.

But I did serve as a Kennedy delegate to the 1960 Democratic National Convention. It happened this way: in 1958 I helped found and served as chairman of Democratic Associates, a Los Angeles area organization of business and professional men. One of our purposes was to meet with contenders for the Presidential nomination. In the fall of 1959, Senator John F. Kennedy spoke to us at a breakfast gathering in the Ambassador Hotel. That was the first time I met him, and I was immensely impressed by this informed, articulate, and patient young man. Kennedy spoke at four other gatherings in the hotel that day. I attended each one, and left a Kennedy supporter, a stand from which I never wavered—in contrast to such California Democrats as Governor Pat Brown, who vacillated so repeatedly during the months before the convention that *Time* magazine called him a "tower of Jello."

I had acquired some party standing as chairman of Democratic Associates and as a member of the Democratic State Finance Committee and of the Chairman's Advisory Committee of the Los Angeles County Democratic Committee. (Indeed, I had gone pretty far to the liberal side for a top officer of a big—Prudential is the third largest corporation in the world—conservative, life insurance company. There were not many business executives who were also active Democrats in the Los Angeles area, and even though Prudential's president was a broad-minded man, there were limits.)

So why was I chosen for public anonymity in the President's Cabinet? I think it was simply that the Kennedy people wanted to include a Californian in the Cabinet and I came as near as anyone to being acceptable to all the factions of the Party in the state.

The corpulent and powerful Kennedy political lieutenant in California, Assemblyman Jesse Unruh, has another idea. He always claimed that I was appointed at his urging. For reasons best known to Unruh, he wanted to keep State Senator Hugo Fisher, whose name had been mentioned in this connection, from the appointment. Unruh has been put out ever since because I did not evidence the gratitude which he thought I owed him.

After President Kennedy was elected, his brother-in-law, Sargent Shriver, telephoned me twice to recruit me into the new

Administration. I told Shriver that it wouldn't be feasible for Kennedy to offer me anything I could accept. When Kennedy did, I accepted, and so began the most hectic five weeks of my life. From the day Senator Kennedy told me of my appointment—December 15, 1960—until the Inauguration on January 20, I did not spend a quiet moment. Those weeks were the most incredibly confused and hectic that I ever expect to live through.

The frantic pace began the evening of December 15, when I flew from Los Angeles to Washington. Awaiting me at the Statler Hotel was a copy of a book written by my predecessor, Arthur Summerfield. I read it the next day while Kennedy and I flew to Palm Beach. My reading matter was noticed, naturally, and duly reported in the press. After the story revealed that I had read Summerfield's book, which some postal employee groups considered too pro-management, my mail began to be overloaded with books, all of them copies of *Mailman—U.S.A.,* an anti-Summerfield book by Bill Doherty, colorful and articulate president of the National Association of Letter Carriers. The tone of his book can best be judged by the fact that he referred to Summerfield throughout as "King Arthur." The books came from letter carriers around the country who wanted me to know the employees' viewpoint.

The President-elect announced my appointment and introduced me to the press on the patio of his father's house in Palm Beach. On that occasion he referred to a letter which had taken eight days to go from Washington to Boston. "I hope Mr. Day will do better," he said. So did I.

I spent the next several days in intimate touch with mail, by which I mean sorting it. Many of the 590,000 postal employees and their employee organizations, members of Congress, major users of the United States mails, Prudential employees, personal friends, and forgotten acquaintances sent letters of congratulation, and if not letters, telegrams. They arrived by the bushel and intermingled with the family Christmas cards and urgent mail. Even with the help of the children, it was difficult to sort out the mail that required an immediate reply from items that could wait.

While the mail arrived at the door, the press was calling on the telephone. *Life* magazine wanted a "human interest" picture of the family for a special article on the new Cabinet. My wife put her foot down when they invited themselves, their cameras, and lighting equipment to our house on Christmas Day to photograph me carving the turkey. Instead, they took some shots of me working on my stamp albums. If they thought I was an avid and active collector, they found out otherwise when my twelve-year-old Jimmy looked at the albums and inquired where they came from, adding gratuitously, "I never saw *them* before."

At the same time another magazine put my wife through a long picture-taking session in the front yard in a variety of costumes for an article on wives of Cabinet officers.

A photographer for a news magazine wanted "just a few minutes" for a color shot of me in the tiny, jammed, temporary office loaned me by the chairman of the Senate Post Office Committee, Olin D. Johnson of South Carolina. The picture took only a few minutes to shoot, all right, but the photographer showed up in my office two hours beforehand to set up his lights and camera, climbing over job-seekers and visitors who tried to shout above the clatter.

Reporters seeking new "human interest" angles even interviewed my fourth grade teacher, Mrs. Hilda Carls of Bluffs, Illinois, and my closest friend from Springfield public school days, Jimmy Sinnott of New Orleans. My ninety-one-year-old father was called by a reporter from the Chicago *Tribune*.

And five books about people in the new Administration were in the works. Each one involved an interview in depth (and length) to produce something new and sparkling.

In the meantime I was winding up my duties with Prudential, but this was complicated by the fact that my close friend and mentor, Prudential president Carrol Shanks, retired just four days after I was designated Postmaster General. Because his successor was not named until many weeks later, and because of some delay in selecting my successor as vice president in charge of the Western Home Office, I continued in that position until Inauguration Day, handling it from Washington after January 2.

And of course, while winding up my old job I wanted to learn something about my new one, inasmuch as I would be appearing before a House subcommittee on the Post Office's four and a half-billion-dollar budget in less than a month after taking office. But it was almost impossible to shake loose from endless picture-taking sessions and interviews.

There would, I was certain, be one great advantage to this public exposure. The series of identity crises with which I had been plagued since arriving in Washington would come to a quick end. I knew that all the interviews and the pictures would remove what last shred of anonymity I now felt that I possessed. If my name were not to become a household word, at least it would be remembered and associated with my face in those households where words (and politics) count.

With this in mind, I sought to capitalize on my anonymity while I still had it, and, in March 1961, I wrote an article for the New York *Times Magazine* about some of the problems of the most unknown Cabinet member.

But the great New York *Times* made a mistake. My picture appeared with the article and under it, big as life, was this caption:

"The 'least known' Cabinet member—J. Clarence Day."

Clarence!

Chapter 2
PULL
HELPS

So I CAME to Washington, unknown and—what's worse—unknowing. Instantly it became clear that there were going to be problems.

Overnight my official family had grown from 7,500 persons at the Prudential to 580,000 Post Office personnel in fifty states—a record not even Abraham would have tried to emulate. I was not long in getting the impression that my friends had suddenly multiplied in like manner. The number and the contents of letters that came to my office amazed me. Acquaintances who ordinarily regarded politics as a roost for rascals and idlers were so overcome at the thought of a friend in the upper reaches of the Federal bureaucracy that they filled my mail with what I came to call "by-the-way" letters. They all began something like this:

"Dear Ed—Congratulations on the great honor that has come to you . . . sacrifice . . . dedication . . . public service . . ." And they concluded on this note: "By the way, I have a brother (husband, cousin, neighbor, friend, business associate) who would like to be appointed Governor of Guam (U. S. Marshal in the Virgin Islands, Federal District Attorney, etc., etc.)."

I never suspected that I had so many friends. They all thought that I was a combination Jim Farley, Boss Tweed, and Santa Claus, dipping into a bottomless pork barrel and dispensing as many jobs as stamps. They all knew me on a first-name basis. (One even addressed me as "Dear Eddy," a name no one calls me.) They all wanted favors. A distant kinsman even wanted to be a federal "consultant on the nutritional problems of chickens," *provided* he could remain in Florida.

7

Nothing, however, in all the thousands of letters I received from friends, acquaintances, and strangers seeking jobs and promotions for themselves or for relatives, approached for sheer brass one by-the-way letter from an officer of a big insurance company. After the usual preliminaries he wrote: "My wife's cousin's husband who is a dentist would like to be postmaster of——because he is tired of commuting to the city."

I wrote back: "I have your letter about your wife's cousin's husband who is a dentist who would like to be a postmaster. You left out a very important piece of information. Does he do extraction work? Because pull helps."

And it does.

From Administrations immemorial the Post Office has been the center of patronage. Even today every vacancy that occurs among the 35,000 postmasters and 33,000 rural letter carriers is filled by political appointment, that is, on the recommendation of the local member of the House of Representatives, if he is of the party that controls the White House, or if he is not, on the recommendation of local officials of the party in the White House. Promotions, too, until I became Postmaster General, depended heavily on political influence.

Because of this intricate system of political rewards and punishments known as patronage, it was the custom for the national party chairman, who was supposed to know who deserved what, to be named Postmaster General so that he could see that they got what they deserved. Arthur Summerfield, whom I succeeded, had been Republican National Chairman during Eisenhower's first campaign for the Presidency. Jim Farley, while serving as PMG during the first eight years of Franklin Roosevelt's Administration, continued as Democratic National Chairman *and* New York State Democratic Chairman. Except for Harry Truman—the only President in history to appoint a career postal official to head the Post Office Department—every President for the thirty years before Kennedy had appointed the national chairman of the party, as had many presidents before that.

Inasmuch as I had no standing in the national party organization and had never dealt with patronage except in a minor way in

my state position, many people—I was among them—concluded
that my appointment as PMG represented a complete departure
from the old pattern. We assumed that no longer would the
political aspects of the Post Office Department be handled by
the principal political manager of the Administration. We were
wrong. The change in 1961 was one of form more than substance,
as I began to realize very soon after becoming PMG.

The chief political manager of the Kennedy Administration
was also very much in charge of the political aspects of the Post
Office Department. That man was not Democratic National
Chairman John Bailey, who was largely a figurehead. The man
in charge of both was Bobby Kennedy, the Attorney General.

He passed on applicants for the top, appointive positions in the
Department. He telephoned in person or sent word through his
staff about certain appointments of postmasters and rural letter
carriers. One afternoon I talked to him three times by telephone
about a single rural letter carrier who was to be appointed in a
small town in Mississippi in which Bobby was intensely interested. He took an occasional interest in appointments to inter-
mediate jobs in the Department and in those who were going to
sell or lease property to the Post Office.

During the flight to Palm Beach on December 16, 1960, with
the President-elect and his brother in the Kennedy family's plane,
both Kennedys briefed me about my new job. Significantly,
Bobby did most of the talking.

When we had a major internal crisis in the Department in
1962, it was Bobby who came over from the Justice Department
personally to straighten the problem out. When a controversy
arose over continuation of a particular one of the Department's
25,000 separate leases, Bobby sent his personal representative to
look into the matter.

When too many members of the White House staff were giving orders to various people in the Post Office Department, it
was decided that the liaison between the two offices should con-
sist of one man. Bob Kennedy named that man.

It should have been clear where the power was, but learning
who doled out the plums of patronage was a hard lesson for

some. The new Democratic State Chairman from a large and populous state visited President Kennedy at the White House. Emerging from the President's office he told a White House staff man that he would now have the final say on Federal patronage in his state. The President had so assured him, he claimed.

"You've got it wrong," the White House staffer said. "All recommendations are to clear through the Attorney General."

Thus it was not so much a departure as it seemed from the old pattern from the Farley days.

In those days the Postmaster General needed the cavernous reception room adjoining his office in order to contain the job-seekers who besieged him. To keep them out of his office the skillful Farley would make an appearance in the grandiose room, give everyone a handshake with a big smile, and before the job-seekers knew what had happened, disappear into his inner office, which was only slightly smaller. In his multifarious political capacities, Farley co-ordinated patronage for all Federal departments and for New York State as well. In other words, a vast number of persons worked—or didn't work—at his pleasure. As there were as many as 16 million persons out of work at one time in those Depression days, the crush in the Postmaster General's reception room was considerable.

Farley made such a profound impression on Washington— a fickle city with a very poor memory for former residents, no matter how famous—that he is remembered well nearly thirty years later.

When I was Postmaster General, a hat-check girl at the Statler Hotel in Washington looked at me quizzically and asked, "Haven't I seen you someplace before?"

"I'm the Postmaster General," I said.

"Farley?" she asked pleasantly.

Postmasters were given civil service status in 1938, during the Farley regime. Lest anyone misunderstand, this was not done for considerations of good government. But by 1938 all the postmasterships had been filled with Democratic appointees. Putting them under civil service insured both their jobs (should the Republicans take over) and, in gratitude, their loyal votes (making a Republican takeover all the less likely).

It is strange that so many prominent members of Congress forget this great accomplishment (whatever the motives behind it) in government. I paid my respects to one such Senator in the weeks before Inauguration Day. Well known for his respect for the civil service and good government generally, the Senator wanted a new postmaster appointed to a large city in his state.

"Why, Senator," I told him, "there's no vacancy there. That postmaster has been confirmed and has civil service protection."

"When did they do that?" he bellowed. In my position I was already learning not to bellow back to members of Congress.

The politically appointed jobs of postmaster and rural letter carrier are the most sought-after jobs in the Federal Government.

Although it carries with it the prestige of the United States, the job of postmaster is seriously underpaid. When I took office in 1961, the salary of the Postmaster of New York City was 17,000 dollars a year, even though he supervised the work of 40,000 employees handling about the same amount of mail each year as the entire British Postal System.

The job is also hard work and no longer the sinecure that it was before 1933. In that year, First Assistant Postmaster General Joseph O'Mahoney, later a United States Senator from Wyoming, decreed that all postmasters had to put in an eight-hour working day. Previously the career employees had done the work in all but the very small offices.

It took a while for the word to get around, however. One applicant for the job approached his Congressman about an appointment.

"I don't know if you can qualify," said the Congressman. "You've got to take a civil service examination and you have to show you have the necessary management experience."

"Hold on there," said the job-seeker. "I said I wanted to be postmaster, not superintendent of mails."

On the other hand, rural letter carrier appointments are often real plums. The pay system for rural carriers was set up on a mileage basis in the days of horse-drawn mail vehicles, muddy roads, and frequent stops at small, family farms. Now the rural carrier, using a modern automobile on paved roads, and with few stops because farms are much larger today, can frequently finish his route by eleven in the morning. On the basis of pay that still prevails, he may receive as much as 10 or even 15 dollars an hour for the actual time he puts in. His salary may be 8,000 or 9,000 dollars a year, with time left over to run a farm, family business, or hold a second job.

This may explain why such positions are so hotly sought after: prestige for the postmaster and a plum for the rural letter carrier.

And of course the filling of these positions generates enormous interest on the very highest levels of government. The theory is that since almost the entire legislative program originates from the White House and the President stakes his prestige on a series of "must bills," the President has to give something to the Congressmen in exchange for their votes. More often than not, that something is patronage.

I disagree with the whole system. I think that as far as possible patronage and politics should be eliminated from the Post Office and that legislation should originate in the Congress itself, not the White House. The President should concentrate on foreign policy and on running the executive branch of the government.

Ultimately, patronage buys very few votes. Congressmen take for granted that their control of appointments of postmasters and rural letter carriers is not a privilege but a right. They do not feel that they owe the White House anything in return for it. They know from experience that no matter how many times a member of Congress of the President's own party votes against the President's bills, he doesn't lose his postal patronage. Similarly, no matter how many times a Republican votes for a Democratic President's bills (or vice versa), he gets none.

Many conscientious Senators and Representatives have no use for the system of postal patronage. Others, some of them very powerful in Congress, can never get enough of it. And they have no hesitation in using it for leverage themselves. For instance, in 1963 the Administration was staking a great deal on getting a bill through Congress. One day a lawmaker telephoned the White House. "In just seven minutes I am going into a committee meeting to vote on that bill," the member said. "Unless I get a promise within those seven minutes that a new post office will be built in my home town, I am not going to vote for it."

Opportunities for such unseemly pressure tactics are created daily by the system of paying for votes in patronage. A promotion for a postal employee or a defense contract for a company in a certain Congressional district is sometimes a small price for one vital vote, the Administration feels.

A first step in de-emphasizing politics in the Post Office would put rural letter carriers in the career system. Now they pack too much political punch in preserving their highly inequitable pay system. They should be given their jobs on the basis of civil service tests, as are forest rangers, food and drug inspectors, and other Federal employees.

I was frequently urged to get Republican postmasters out of office, which could have meant harassing them with investigations and various trumped-up charges. I always refused to do so. During my first year in office only 70 of 35,000 postmasters were removed. As many of them were Democrats as Republicans and the charges against each were of an extremely serious nature.

Those who urged me to this course of action never quite said that they were asking me to undermine—indeed, violate—the Civil Service Law. Had I been so unscrupulous, it would not have worked. It was tried before, but it failed.

In that era charges were made against the postmaster of a large office. He fought the effort to remove him and, after a hearing, he won. He was so elated that he went out to celebrate. He had a few drinks, was arrested for drunken driving, and was fired the next day.

Politics even rears its unsightly head in the elite corps of the Post Office Department, the Postal Inspection Service. This group of career men is selected entirely from the ranks of postal clerks and letter carriers to play a role demanding unimpeachable integrity. Before the men are chosen, however, their political affiliation is recorded in the personnel files so that a political balance may be maintained. In addition, the higher officials of the Postal Inspection Service, both in its Department headquarters and in its 15 divisions, tend to be chosen largely from members of the Service who belong to the party in power.

The Service is extremely powerful. Its unfavorable report can result in the removal of a postmaster, thus creating a vacancy and a patronage appointment. Therefore it is most unfortunate that in this Service, whose integrity must be unquestioned and whose *esprit de corps* is very strong, there should be a subtle aroma of politics.

Besides personnel, there is another aspect of Post Office operations that adds to the strong political flavor of the department. About 1,000 new post office buildings are completed each year. The announcement that each one is to be built is handled to give maximum credit and publicity to the local Representative, provided he is a member of the Party controlling the White House. Otherwise, the announcement is made through a United States Senator or even through the Governor of the state. What's essential is that the announcement build up some office-holder of the party in power.

The fragrance that hangs over the Post Office is indeed pungently political, even under a nonpolitical Postmaster General. Fortunately that aspect of the Department was not in my sphere of influence. And it is consoling to know that it used to be much worse.

During Abraham Lincoln's time there was no such thing as a Civil Service and Lincoln, while worrying about the Civil War, was subjected to endless harassment from job-seekers. He originated most of the anecdotes still current about dispensing patronage.

Nearly every Congressman in Washington will tell you that when he gets someone appointed to a Federal job, he makes one ingrate and twenty enemies. Lincoln said it first.

During Lincoln's trip to Gettysburg to make his famous address, he contracted a serious and contagious fever. That did not deter the job-seekers, who tried to see him anyway.

"Let them all come in," said Lincoln to his secretary. "At last I have something I can give everyone."

Chapter 3
FOWL
PLAY

NOT EVERYONE with pull wants a job. Political pressure on the Post Office can take many forms, some of them unusual indeed. Take the case of the overstuffed fowl. That was in 1948, when the Post Office issued a stamp bearing a picture of an obese hen to honor the 100th anniversary of the poultry industry.

How it was calculated that the poultry industry was founded in 1848, since people were raising chickens in the days of the Pharaohs, will remain forever a mystery. What was perfectly clear was that the chicken stamp represented the absolute low point in postal subject matter. Applicants for new stamps still point to it to show that by comparison their subject is much more deserving.

This particular travesty doubtless came about because of the hard work of a fowl lobbyist. In 1948 stamp subjects were chosen by Congress, which would pass a bill calling for a specific commemorative to be issued. Usually these bills generated little interest, except on the part of lobbyists for obscure causes. But once passed, the only way such a demand from Congress could be rejected was for the President to veto it, which of course he was reluctant to do.

When it became known that a chicken stamp would be issued, thousands of collectors of "first day covers" began to search for an appropriate place from which to issue it. At last a tiny post office with a singularly apt postmark was discovered in the wilds of Alaska. It was named Chicken.

With typical diligence the Post Office Department rushed a postal inspector to Chicken to make the necessary preparations.

He had some difficulty finding the place at all. When he finally arrived, he found that the post office consisted of a few feet of counter space at the back of a cluttered general store. On the counter was a box of stamps. Customers took what they wanted from the box and left cash in return. There were also some money order forms and a box for mail, which came in at irregular intervals.

The postal inspector explained to the postmaster, who was also a storekeeper and notary public, that great things were about to happen in Chicken. Soon thousands of requests for first day cancellations would be pouring in from all over the world, the inspector said. The requests would be accompanied by large amounts of money to pay for the new chicken stamps, so naturally his somewhat informal accounting arrangements would have to be improved. And it was very important that the stamps should be glued carefully on the envelopes, and that each envelope should be postmarked by hand so that the cancellations would be perfectly straight and low enough not to deface the stamps. All these procedures might entail some inconvenience for the postmaster, the inspector conceded, but this stamp would put Chicken on the map! The postal inspector went on in this way, painting a glowing picture of what was about to happen to Chicken.

The postmaster listened, incredulous. When the inspector finally finished, the postmaster picked up a gunny sack, put into it the box of stamps, the box of incoming letters, the money order forms and the postmarker bearing the name of Chicken. Handing the sack to the inspector, he said, "Here's your post office. I resign."

With the chicken stamp firmly in mind, in 1962 I faced a delegation that had come to plead the cause of another and equally ridiculous commemorative stamp.

I shall always remember this group. In accordance with standard operating procedure their Congressman had made the appointment and promised to meet them in my office, but at the last minute he "couldn't make it."

The leader of the delegation was a man I had never met in my life, but when he was ushered into my office he greeted me effusively as "old friend Ed." When I tried to shake hands with him, he threw his arm around my shoulders and retained this affectionate and familiar pose while introducing me to the others. He then inquired with great solicitude about my family, although the only way he could have known that I had a family was by hearsay.

After these lengthy preliminaries, he began to edge into the build-up for his stamp. The suggestion was familiar, and completely out of the question. The stamp didn't come close to fitting the Department's established subject requirements. Therefore I carefully explained the rules and said no.

They all began to talk at once, offering every kind of argument. One said, "But the Department issued a stamp once for a subject similar to this."

"Yes," I said. "Nearly every ridiculous thing that could be put on a stamp has appeared on United States Postage one time or another. But I'm not bound to repeat all the blunders of the past."

Then, chuckling amiably, I came up with what I thought was my clincher:

"Why, do you realize that the Department once issued a stamp with a picture of a big fat hen on it to honor *chickens?*"

"What's wrong with that?" erupted a member of the delegation. "The chicken industry is one of the greatest industries in the United States."

The gentleman, it turned out, had been Commissioner of Agriculture in a large Eastern state. In that capacity he had developed an inordinate fondness for fowl. Or else poultry breeders raised a lot of votes.

Over the years the Post Office Department has had many problems concerning chickens, mostly because day-old chicks may be sent through the mails. Not long ago a rural letter carrier in New England was trying to deliver a carton of them. He couldn't find anyone at home, tried all the doors with no success, and finally, to avoid leaving the chicks outdoors unattended, he opened the carton and dropped the chicks one by one through the mail slot in the front door! According to Postal Regulations he should have auctioned them off promptly in the post office lobby, but regulations are sometimes hard to conform to. It was considerably harder, though, to pacify that farmer's wife.

Lest I be thought to pick on chickens, let me say that other subjects for commemorative stamps have been urged on the Post Office which aroused the same negative response.

Once we were asked to issue a stamp honoring the 100th anniversary of the pretzel industry. In a speech some time later I suggested that we would be glad to issue a pretzel stamp if only someone could come up with a glue for it that would taste like beer. (I once repeated that remark in an informal speech to a small group after "dinner at Antoine's" in New Orleans. A whimsical brewery owner, among those present, jumped to his feet and said: "Mr. Day, I have the solution to your problem. Our beer tastes like glue!")

My remarks spoofing the pretzel stamp proposal received some publicity.

In due course I heard from the head of a large pretzel company in Pennsylvania. He wrote a lengthy and irate letter to convince me that the pretzel industry was indeed highly important to the economy, to the nation's nibblers, and to him. Furthermore, statistics showed—and he reeled off a string of them—that more pretzels were eaten with ice cream and cola drinks than with beer, depressing statistics if ever I heard any. It was clear that pretzels were not to be spoofed. For emphasis he sent along a large container of them, twisted into all shapes and sizes.

One puzzling request was received from a number of persons, including Members of Congress, who wanted a stamp to honor the 200th anniversary of the massacre at Fort Michilimackinac *and* the invention of lacrosse. It seemed an extraordinary combination. Then we learned that after failing to penetrate the fort on the day of the massacre the Indians had produced long-handled rackets and begun playing an interesting looking game of ball. More curious than cautious, the inhabitants of the stockade trooped out to watch and, engrossed in the game now called lacrosse, were massacred. All the same, the combination still seemed startling and the message a bit long for one small stamp.

In one year the Post Office Department was urged to issue commemorative stamps to promote the preservation of the totem pole, celebrate the installation of the three thousandth swimming pool in Palm Springs, California, mark the passing of the prehistoric dinosaur in America, eulogize Whooda Tom as the country's supreme hog caller, and immortalize the American hamburger.

As for swimming pools, we felt that they had already gotten enough publicity in the Kennedy Administration.

To the hamburger people, my brilliant special assistant, Jim Kelleher, who handled stamp requests, sent a letter saying that we had chewed their suggestion over but decided to put it on the back burner.

To the others, we just said no.

There are, of course, many ways to say no in public office. One of the most common is to listen at length to all the favorable arguments, accept with enthusiasm all the inevitable brochures, and assure the supplicants that their suggestions will be given the most thorough and sympathetic study. After they leave, instruct someone else in the office to write them in a few days and say that longstanding policy, etc., prevents the granting of their request.

Another technique is to stall until you've seen how much pressure will build up or whether any important member of Congress is *really* interested. He is if he telephones or comes to see you; a letter means absolutely nothing. Likely as not a Congressman writes a letter so that he's got a carbon copy to mail to his constituent. When the late J. Ham Lewis, Senator from Illinois, was urged to recommend a constituent for a job, he would dictate a flowery and enthusiastic letter to the head of the department concerned and mail the carbon to the job-seeker. The original he would throw in the wastebasket.

Taking the affirmative is another matter. Oddly enough it always provokes a negative response. When early in 1963 my slogan ("What this country needs is a good 5-cent stamp.") had paid off and the postage rate for letters was raised, we decided to put Washington's picture on the new stamp. (Since the first United States postage stamps were issued in 1847, it has been usual for the Nation's first president to appear on the most frequently used stamp.) Until 1963 the seldom used 5-cent stamp had borne the picture of our fifth president, James Monroe.

The proposed substitution was no sooner announced (not long after the Cuban missile crisis) than editorials and letters poured into the Department, angrily charging that the change confirmed that the Administration had abandoned the Monroe Doctrine. When the stamp appeared, a lady protested that Washington appeared to be naked. The figure, based on the famed Houdon bust, shows only head and shoulders. Fortunately the protest did not reach the dimensions of the furor caused some years ago when three fulsome females from a Botticelli painting adorned a Pan American Union commemorative. Many irate individuals, their sensibilities grievously affronted, wrote to complain that the three maidens were too scantily clad.

Almost every new stamp or coin has been the subject of rumors that its design was in error or in some way objectionable, and that the offending item would be withdrawn from circulation. After the Jefferson nickel was minted it was widely reported that it would be discontinued because the designer had failed to put a flagpole on Monticello—which has in fact never had a flagpole. When the Pony Express commemorative came out, a host of "experts" from jockeys to veterinarians kicked up a storm of publicity from their charges that a horse could not run—or even stay right side up—in the position shown on the stamp. When the Post Office honored the 75th anniversary of the first transcontinental railroad on a postage stamp, the smoke from the locomotive was shown blowing in one direction and the flag in the opposite. And of course this brought forth the usual flurry of rumors, denials, public criticism, and so forth.

Someone can be found to object to anything. The Daughters of the American Revolution were heard to rumble when foreigners—Garibaldi, Masaryk, Ernst Reuter, and others—appeared on the Champions of Liberty series of stamps, causing one to wonder how Lafayette, Pulaski, and Von Steuben fit into the DAR's concept of Revolutionary history. Various super-patriots raise a hue and cry whenever the American flag appears in the design of a stamp, their theory being that canceling the stamp desecrates the flag. It is safe to state as a general rule of government that every positive action will generate a corresponding negative reaction, and the converse is also true.

So it's a great relief, every now and then, to hear from a harmless eccentric with a simple request, especially when it can be answered as easily as this letter from a Massachusetts man to his Representative. The Massachusetts man wanted a stamp to be issued bearing his picture, "to honor me as the author of a book of poems, a copy of which is in the Eisenhower Library in Abilene, Kansas." He was considerate enough to enclose a photograph of himself reduced to stamp size and perforated. Any denomination would do, he said.

As is the case in these matters, his Congressman sent the letter to me with a request for material for a reply. I repeated the rule: A living person cannot appear on the postage of the United States.

Clearly the best course of action for his constituent was to drop dead, but I hesitated to make this suggestion to the Congressman. Would that the men in appointive positions could be as frank with those in elective positions as is the reverse!

Or as frank as they are with each other, for that matter. Back in the days when Congress chose the subjects for commemorative stamps, a Texas Representative came upon the chairman of the House Post Office Committee in the washroom. "I want to talk to you about a proposal for a new stamp," said the Texan. "It's very important."

"I'm so sick of hearing about these stamp requests," said the chairman. "Why, do you know some damn fool wants a stamp to honor Angora goats?"

"That's my stamp," the gentleman from Texas spluttered. His proposal was not heard again.

But what makes the Postmaster General's relationship with Members of Congress tricky at best is not the stamps that they choose, but those that they use. Or don't use. Riding herd on the use of Congressmen's free mailing privileges is about as prickly a job as a Federal official can have, comparable to having to question the expense account of your boss.

Anything reprinted from the Congressional Record can be mailed, free, no matter how partisan or insignificant its content. This accounts in part for some of the silly items dumped each day into the Appendix to the Record. (Lobbying in one form or another accounts for the rest. In a single week I saw one speech, made by an obscure "civic leader," reprinted five times at the request of five Congressmen, no doubt acting at the request of the man who made the speech. And not long ago a Senator placed in the Record a glowing tribute to a business executive. In his haste he also included the letter from the executive's public relations man suggesting the whole thing.) Anything that can be construed as official can also be mailed free. This accounts for some strange behavior in the political animal.

An extremely conservative Representative, who since his defeat works full time for the John Birch Society, once sent a mimeographed "Christmas greeting" to thousands of his constituents in Southern California. In a feeble gesture toward giving the greetings some official content he had a list of Cabinet members printed on the reverse side. Naturally he used his free mailing privilege. I think I would have let this pass, but a newspaper columnist wrote it up as if it were a major crime. Shortly thereafter the Representative paid more than 700 dollars in postage.

Free mail is the subject of bitter strife between the House and the Senate. House members want their free mailing privileges broadened to make it easier for them to send out cheap statewide mailings should they decide to run for the Senate. Naturally the Senators, who aren't anxious to give up their seats to overeager Representatives, want the free mail privilege limited.

In 1962 the House and Senate fought bitterly over this issue, holding up bills and issuing angry attacks on one another. In the last hours of the final day of that session of Congress the House attached the free mail provision it wanted to an important appropriations bill and then adjourned for the year. The Senate had to swallow this bitter pill from the House or else bring both Houses of Congress back in special session. The Senate passed the bill, but its fury had been aroused. The following year the Senate blocked the free mail provision of the House for many months. Then Congressman Tom Steed took revenge. He announced that a Senator, whose name he might possibly reveal, had two call girls on his office payroll and that various other Senators were enjoying generous supplies of gift liquor. No names were ever mentioned, the House got the mail provision it wanted, and Washington indulged in one of its biggest rumor games to date.

Chapter 4
THE RUMOR
MANEUVER

ALTHOUGH I enjoyed Washington thoroughly from the start, in one respect I felt like an outsider. I did not take part in the popular game so enjoyed by newsmen and endured, if not always positively relished, by government officials: the rumor maneuver.

The play begins with a report that such and such Federal official is about to resign. The proper response is invariably a denial. Whether he is in fact about to resign is not of primary importance, although extra points are given the newsman for a rumor that turns out to be true, just as they are given for correctly predicting the successor to the office in question. If the rumor proves false, the official gets the points.

The object of the game for both rumorer and rumored-about is to give the report as wide a circulation as possible, preferably nationwide circulation through a syndicated column or wire service. This can be done by (1) repeating (denying) the rumor often enough, (2) reciting (discrediting) the rumor loud enough, or (3) making it fantastic enough (maintaining enigmatic silence about it).

For months and months none of this happened to me. Not only was I left out of touch football, I was also left off the rumor roster. Then it happened. The first rumor appeared, swelled and gave rise to a deluge that did not subside until I did actually resign.

I heard that I was going to return to Illinois to run for office, although I hadn't lived in Illinois in ten years. (Pierre Salinger hadn't shown then that that made no difference.) I heard that I was going to be replaced by a former senator, a former mayor, at least two former governors—in fact, almost any former Democratic official at all, with the exception of Harry Truman. I began to feel that anyone with Party standing who hadn't been named as the next Postmaster General should file a protest with the Equal Opportunity Commission on the grounds that he was being discriminated against. Indeed, the press was providing me with more departures from Washington than the Eastern Airlines shuttle to New York.

But at least I was an outsider no longer. I could play the rumor game with the best of them.

Perhaps it seems that the Washington preoccupation with this sort of thing reaches fantastic proportions, and indeed it does. The press has an almost endless capacity to feed on its own reports and thrive in the process. The press in Washington is also extremely powerful, and it likes to flex its muscles every now and then. And the press in Washington is omnipresent.

In the spring of 1963, when the racial storm was beginning to blow up hard, I was standing with a small group at a cocktail party. Someone asked, "Do you know what NAACP stands for?"

We bit.

"Never Antagonize Adam Clayton Powell."

When a Senator joined our group a little later, I repeated the story. The next day a story on the society page began: "Postmaster General J. Edward Day has this new definition for NAACP . . ." A disconcerting experience, perhaps, but a frequent one in Washington, where almost any idle remark is likely to be quoted in the newspaper next morning. I learned later that the Senator was the culprit in this case. What had happened was that he left the party I was attending, where there were no reporters, for a dinner at which there were several. He repeated the story several times, each time attributing it to me.

The society pages of Washington newspapers are unique. In their columns you will find which prominent persons attended what reasonably newsworthy events the night before and, if space is sufficient, what they had on and what, if anything, was served. But this is not what gains these pages their fame. What you'll find there that you won't find on any other society pages in the country is a report of what was said. Considering that the guests at any Washington function that's worth reporting are almost certain to include a few of the more prominent members of House and Senate, several Ambassadors, a Cabinet member or two, a delegation from the White House staff, groups from various executive departments of the government, and assorted lobbyists, hangers-on and perhaps even a Central Intelligence agent— considering this assortment of people, the resulting conversations will be interesting indeed.

And what the guests talked about the night before is all there the morning after, preserved by those stylish recorders of events who write for the Washington society pages. Along with the description of the decor, a dialogue between VIPs on Vietnam; with the hors d'oeuvres, an Assistant Secretary of State on nuclear testing; and over by the bar, the government official who is reliably (always reliably) reported on his way out. No wonder then that the pages are so fascinating and such a source of information on the issues of the day.

Indeed, the most accurate newspaper account I saw of a controversial proposal I was pushing was a report of my conversation about it at a party, covered, of course, by a society writer. City desk reporters have grown lazy, spoiled by the plethora of publicity handouts that come pouring out of the city's mimeograph machines before and after every speech, announcement, or action. They rely too much on the handout. But a clever society page writer like the *Evening Star*'s Betty Beale can absorb a conversation without taking a note, and report it accurately.

Sometimes the coverage is altogether too accurate for some tastes. Miss Beale was a guest at a big outdoor party at Bobby Kennedy's Virginia estate. She reported in depth about the guests who landed fully clothed in the pool. Bobby was irked no end.

At another occasion, Lee Udall, attractive wife of the Secretary of the Interior, noticed a society reporter busily taking notes. "Please don't report that I have on this same red dress again tonight," she said. The newspaper, of course, carried the exact quote, just as it did when a reporter outside my house asked my son Jimmy where I was.

"Oh, he's inside listening to Radio Moscow on the radio he was given in Japan," said Jimmy. It was true enough, all right, but I would rather not have read it in the Washington *Post* the next morning.

I have always kept in mind a line about official life in Washington, "Never do anything you wouldn't want to see written up on the front page of the New York *Times*." But in truth, most of us in Washington worried less about the front page of the New York *Times*, where we would appear most infrequently, than about the women's pages of the *Post* or the *Star*, where whatever slight indiscretions we might have committed in an unguarded moment were likely to be reported at length.

Newspaper photographers have a special sort of mission, too, and that is to catch public officials in the most candid of poses. It's not the straight head shot that these photographers seek, but the picture of the official pulling his ear, or with a hole in his shoe, or with his mouth wide open about to take a bite of food. A *Life* magazine photographer once spent half an hour in my office taking at least fifty candid shots of me at work. When he seemed to be through, I lit a cigar. The picture that appeared in the magazine made me look like a typical, cigar-puffing politician. But I should have known. And at least I wasn't licking stamps, which seemed to be the goal of most of those who came around to take my picture.

I never believed it was a good policy to argue with or try to punish a newsman who wrote a story I disapproved of, but some very important Washington officials don't feel that way. Speaker of the House John McCormack once showed me some of the voluminous correspondence in which he berated newsmen for saying things about him that he didn't like. The newsman has a job to do and it seldom involves going out of his way to be kind to a public official. Furthermore, the newsman holds most of the trump cards.

It was a member of the press who discovered one day, before I took over the Post Office Department, that I had written a novel. Perhaps he found the information in my biography in *Who's Who*, where it had been hiding all along. At any rate he found a copy of the book and was apparently surprised to find therein characters of both sexes, because he wrote a story suggesting that the book was "spicy."

Instantly the defenders of motherhood and morality fell to lamenting. Republican National Committee Chairman and 1964 Vice-Presidential candidate William Miller leaped into the breach and filled it with press releases. The outraged Miller questioned whether the writer of a "sexy" book was qualified to keep salacious material out of the mails. Probably I sat around reading dirty books, when I wasn't writing them.

The wickedness of my novel, *Bartholf Street,* can best be judged from the manner in which it was prepared for publication. I wrote the novel during World War II, primarily to while away the time during long convoy trips across the Atlantic. When my destroyer escort came into port, I would mail pages of longhand home, where my mother would type them. She was not the kind of woman who read dirty books.

Bartholf Street was intended for serialization in a magazine such as *Cosmopolitan,* but *Cosmopolitan* didn't agree. It was finally published in 1947 to no special literary acclaim. My final royalty payment arrived in 1949. It was 40 cents in stamps.

Indeed, the book was never a hot item (economically *or* thematically) until the flurry of sensational publicity that blew up around it in January, 1961. Then its publisher began a frantic search through his archives, plans were voiced to bring it out in paperback editions, and so on. More than a hundred persons signed up to wait their turn for it at the Library of Congress, the only place in Washington where the book could be obtained.

Of course, that was when everybody thought they were in for another *Lady Chatterley's Lover.* But the incident does illustrate the power of the press. Or the pull of pornography. And as Postmaster General I would be hearing a lot about both.

Chapter 5
LADY CHATTERLEY'S
WHAT?

THERE never was a man who dedicated himself more thoroughly or more publicly to keeping literature decent and the mails unsullied than Mr. Arthur Summerfield, my predecessor.

When his eye chanced to fall across the sullied pages of *Lady Chatterley's Lover,* the resulting exclamations and protests reverberated through the Post Office to the White House, the Federal courts, and the nation. It was widely reported in Washington that in the course of his campaign to keep the book out of the mails he even sent President Eisenhower an annotated copy with the offending passages underlined.

No doubt Mr. Miller's righteous indignation when he learned that I had written a novel was closely related to Mr. Summerfield's outbursts against *Lady Chatterley's Lover.* (Of course, Summerfield had read *Lady Chatterley.*) In the Chatterley case, when the judicial officer of the Post Office Department refused to sign an order banning the book from the mails, he was relieved of his job. The order got signed but the Federal District Court and the Federal Court of Appeals held that the order was improper. Despite Summerfield's urging, the Department of Justice refused to take *Lady Chatterley* to the Supreme Court. The book became a best seller, probably because of all the efforts to suppress it.

Mr. Summerfield's zeal and enthusiasm for postal purity was boundless. In his vigilant pursuit of pornography he encouraged the use of a postal cancellation die that urged Americans to *Report obscene material to your postmaster.* Some people objected to this injunction, however well intentioned, when it was

29

emblazoned across the envelopes of their Christmas greetings or their children's Valentines, and when I became Postmaster General the die was cast, but out.

With it went Summerfield's Chamber of Horrors, as all Washington called the museum he maintained in a locked room adjacent to his office. It contained copious amounts of what you were supposed to report to your postmaster. Visiting vigilantes were escorted through it. Members of Congress, reporters, presidents of men's clubs, presidents of women's clubs and any number of members thereof, all trouped through Summerfield's famed museum. Its exhibits were arranged by specialty in the various perversions. Presumably they inspired a militant attitude against the purveyors of pornography.

I was intensely interested in a more effective crackdown on pornography, but I did not want to exhibit it or make speeches about it, so I closed the Chamber of Horrors and either destroyed its contents or returned the stuff to the files of the Chief Inspector, where it belonged. I considered it more important to act against obscenity in the mails from a solid, legal base, than to raise a hullabaloo. During my first fiscal year in office both arrests and convictions for violations went up 33 per cent over the previous year. Publicity went down more than proportionately.

One year we got 25,000 complaints about two items put out by a New York publisher, who hoped that I would take mild action through Department procedures to try to ban his smut from the mails. This would have resulted in lengthy litigation, which he didn't especially want, but the litigation would have drawn lots of publicity, which he wanted very much. We got him indicted under the criminal laws instead, and he was found guilty on all counts. We were less successful in stopping another promotion campaign for dubious material. We prevented its being mailed in bulk from Intercourse, Pennsylvania, but the promoter sent it out instead under a Middlesex, New Jersey, postmark.

At any rate, after I closed Summerfield's museum ladies who were active in various clean literature groups around the country protested because I would not supply them with samples of obscenity so that they could convince prospective members of the urgency of the problem. I don't think anybody needs to take dope to determine the seriousness of the narcotics problem, and the same principle holds true for pornography. It really doesn't take one to know one, as they say.

When I discontinued the "obscene material" cancellation die, an "acting" postmaster in San Diego, California, who knew he was not going to be made permanent, called in the press and announced that he could not bring himself to stay on under Post Office leadership whose tactics openly encouraged the dissemination of pornography. He stated that obscene literature was "a weapon of the Communists for undermining our American moral fibre." Morally fibrous himself, he generously consented to stay on in his job until his successor was appointed. As it turned out, that took fifteen minutes.

Comment on the matter in the local press included a cartoon showing two men talking about me. One was saying, "I understand this fellow Day actually practices philately—and there's a good chance he may eventually become a complete sexagenarian."

When I dismantled the Museum of Postal History, another of Mr. Summerfield's educational endeavors, and sent it to the Smithsonian Institution because we needed the space it occupied for offices, nobody claimed that I was opposed to history. I couldn't understand why.

My predecessor and his museums were not the only things to leave the Post Office when I moved in. Behind the Postmaster General's desk hung a huge portrait of Ike. The painting had been placed so that whenever Summerfield was photographed, Ike appeared to be peering approvingly over his shoulder, bestowing benisons. The picture made the office, woodpaneled and of a grandeur to satisfy President de Gaulle, look like precinct headquarters. Ike was removed and the large painting of Benjamin Franklin, first Postmaster General, restored to its position in the panel behind my desk. I also brought in a handsome portrait of William Barry of Kentucky, the first Postmaster General to be a member of the Cabinet and the man (a Democrat) under whom Abraham Lincoln served as postmaster (in New Salem, Illinois, at an annual salary of 55 dollars). I hung the

Howard Chandler Christie portrait of Jim Farley and, for a bipartisan touch, a painting of John Wanamaker, Republican merchant, postmaster of Philadelphia, and later Postmaster General.

To complete the collection I borrowed a portrait of the first Adlai Ewing Stevenson from the public library in Bloomington, Illinois. Stevenson was First Assistant Postmaster General in Cleveland's first Administration and Vice President in his second. When Cleveland, a Democrat, took office after twenty-five years of Republican rule, Stevenson's assignment was to relieve thousands of Republican appointees from their jobs. He performed these duties so effectively that he became known—not too endearingly—as The Hatchet. I hung the Stevenson portrait more as a tribute to his famous grandson, whose public service has been vastly more idealistic, than as a portent of things to come in the Post Office Department.

All play with pictures, whether from personal whim or political motive, I grouped in a broad classification known as the portrait ploy. In the office of the Postmaster General there is a great deal of space in which to indulge this activity. That office is the largest in Washington, big enough to accommodate an indoor tennis court. (When the present Interior Department building was going up, Secretary Harold Ickes was said to have ordered that his office be one foot longer than the Postmaster General's, giving him the largest office in town. Observation shows that the order, if given, was never carried out.) After buzzing for my secretary I always felt that I should give her ten minutes lead time so that she wouldn't have to sprint what seemed like the half-mile from the door to my desk.

Outside the Postmaster General's grandiose office is a baronial hall which was Farley's reception room. It is even bigger than the office, with great marble floors and vast high ceilings. It has always seemed to me like a lobby looking for a hotel. And its ample wall space almost cries for portraits.

When I first visited these quarters during the transition period, Mr. Summerfield was eager to give me a tour of the place, with special attention to the portraits of past incumbents. In the reception room we stopped before one picture. "Who is that?" I asked. I should have known, of course, but I was preoccupied.

"It's me," said a somewhat miffed Summerfield.

You can't tell much about Post Office history from the pictures. After many inquiries about an oil portrait in a particularly elaborate gilt frame, I learned that it was a likeness of an Assistant Postmaster General who had been in office three months in the 1880's. He must have spent most of that time posing for his portrait.

One version of the portrait ploy uses autographed photographs instead of oil portraits, and takes place at intervals in most of the country's post offices. The Postmaster General's signed photograph is in great demand by postmasters throughout the country who exhibit it as a sign of favor from above. These requests were a little disconcerting at first. In my recollection, pictures in post office lobbies always bore in very large, black letters the word WANTED.

Many postmasters in the hinterlands haven't attained the skill with pictures which officials in Washington, used to surviving near the center of the maelstrom, have acquired. They just don't play the game well enough or fast enough, and the walls of many postmasters' offices I visited had glaring white patches where, quite obviously, quite recently, and quite foolishly, pictures of political and postal officials from the Eisenhower Administration had been removed.

Still, I cannot think of a more brilliant practitioner of the picture ploy than a clerk in the damaged parcel disposal section of the San Francisco Post Office. He was apparently a natural genius, inasmuch as he had never worked in Washington where he might have been expected to develop this ability. Now it so happened, when I was Western Vice President for Prudential, that I would occasionally send an autographed picture to a sales manager in a field office. In the summer of 1960 I sent one to our Fresno manager with the inscription, "To Jim Simovaklis, with best wishes from Ed Day."

The picture was damaged in transit and had been discarded when, after I was appointed Postmaster General, this postal clerk noticed it in a pile of debris. He carefully applied ink eradicator to the words "To Jim Simovaklis," and displayed prominently at his place of work a smiling picture of me signed, "with best wishes from Ed Day."

In the long run, however, pictures count for very little. The acting postmaster of Gettysburg, Pennsylvania, had on his wall a photograph of Ike that the General had inscribed with a warm, personal message. But he was only acting postmaster because the Republican Senator from Pennsylvania would not agree to his confirmation, and Senatorial courtesy is a powerful force that often transcends party lines.

A variant on the portrait ploy has to do with plaques. Nothing is so ludicrous in an administration changeover in the Post Office as the hubbub over whose names should appear on which bronze plaques in new post offices. As more than a thousand post office buildings are constructed each year, there were a number in various stages of completion on January 30, 1961, plus some already finished but not yet occupied, and others that had been occupied but were not yet formally dedicated. Those that had been dedicated before January 20 had—and kept—plaques bearing the names of President Eisenhower and his Postmaster General. The rest caused problems.

In the entire history of our country I doubt that a voter has been swayed because he saw or did not see a particular name emblazoned on cornerstone or plaque, or otherwise immortalized on a public building at taxpayers' expense. But precedent was against me. The cornerstone of the Post Office Department's Washington headquarters, laid in 1932, bears the names of Herbert Hoover and a baker's dozen of his officials (including Walter Brown, Hoover's Postmaster General who spent 9,000 dollars of his own money for a special limousine with a roof high enough to accommodate him and his top hat). But by the time construction proceeded to the first floor of the Post Office Building, the Administration had changed and an entire marble wall is carved with the names of the new group: Roosevelt, Farley, and a generous assortment of lesser fry. Similarly, Hoover Dam, under F.D.R., became Boulder Dam. After 1952, it was back to Hoover Dam again.

Because at first I did not get perturbed about plaques, the situation got quite out of hand. In the Senate, Everett Dirksen made a speech about the great issue of whose names should appear on the bronze tablet in the new post office in Galesburg, Illinois. In Cincinnati, the local people insisted that Eisenhower's name should appear on the new Robert A. Taft Post Office Station, even though the building was occupied and dedicated after President Kennedy took office. And in little Monroe, Iowa, the post office was never dedicated at all. It had been built under the Republicans, but was to be dedicated under the Democrats at a ceremony attended by Republican Representative John Henry Kyl. On the façade of this post office a plaque bearing the names of Dwight David Eisenhower and his coterie had been placed, a bit prematurely. Several days before the ceremony, however, a John F. Kennedy plaque was substituted for the Eisenhower plaque. Mr. Kyl insisted that the Ike plaque be restored. Thus it came to my attention, and, desperately sick of the whole business, I had the Kennedy plaque removed. But I wasn't going to have any more foolishness. The hole was plugged up, and the dedication canceled. That's one post office without a plaque.

One bright note in all this plaque yak was a letter from a Democratic leader in Texas. "This new building is so poorly located, so inconveniently arranged, and so lacking in any parking lot except a large mudhole, that even though it was completed and occupied after our Administration took office I insist you equip it with an Eisenhower-Summerfield plaque prominently displayed."

Plaque yak, the portrait ploy, and related diversions tend to foster VIP Fever in those susceptible to the malady, which results from confusing the importance of the office with one's own importance. The strong appetite for personal glorification that characterizes the affliction is manifested in various symptoms: the contented smile through the repetitious and unctuous accolades during testimonial dinners; the greedy amassing of innumerable awards, plaques, and scrolls which later appear on the office wall; lengthy sittings for portraits to be left for the pleasure of posterity and successors to the office; self-praise by press release, and so on.

Characteristic, too, of the condition, is that its victim does not suffer—he loves it—but those around him do. One official of the Eisenhower Administration sat front row center in a convention hall while subordinates in his agency put on a two-hour pageant praising his accomplishments. The 58-page script was heavily laced with directions for organ crescendos, trumpet fanfares, spotlights playing on the great man himself, and electric fans strategically placed to cause the American flags to flutter at designated moments. The high point of the production was an ecstatic statement describing the object of all the attention as "the man with the golden viscera."

I puzzled over this line for some time before the meaning of the anatomical accolade became clear: it was an effort to link his 24-carat character with the concept of a man with guts.

He had a fairly rare and truly awesome case of the malady, but less severe attacks are common. It always amazes me to see prominently displayed on the office wall of a supposedly sophisticated executive a framed certificate from some airline, attesting to the fact that the executive has, by having flown 100,000 miles, attained the honorary rank of "Ambassador," or "Charter Flight Customer," or "Red Carpet Club Member." I would as soon hang up a certificate saying that I had accumulated and redeemed a hundred books of Green Stamps.

When I sought to stem the tide of tribute that pours into the offices of Government officials by telling a banquet group that I was "allergic to plaques," they interpreted my remark to mean that I wanted something fancier, and I received for my desk an expensive engraved medallion enclosed in a large block of clear plastic.

Of course, public officials have to get some satisfaction out of their Government service. And some are satisfied with plaques.

Others, like my predecessor, while not disdaining plaques, really prefer the printed record. In February, 1961, the transition issue of the Postal Service News, an official journal put out for the Department's 580,000 employees and financed by the taxpayers, was ready for distribution. Because this was the transition issue, it was supposed to be nonpolitical. Just before resigning, however, Summerfield made over the issue so that it featured a large picture of himself together with a full-page letter of praise from President Eisenhower. He also inserted his "final report" to the President, although the Postal Service News seemed a strange place in which to make it. He reported that the Post Office now faced the future with confidence, which was good news to me.

Some copies of the News had already been mailed when I heard about the issue. I was quite amused, and was not inclined to do anything about the Summerfield "testimonial" issue. But aides urged me to halt distribution because, they said, some employees might think it signified that the policies of the previous eight years were to continue. We weren't sure that that was the image we wanted to present.

Chapter 6
FROM A(BCD)
TO Z(IP)

AFTER I had hung the portraits, disposed of the museums, perused Mr. Summerfield's final report, and learned to find my way to the desk at the far end of my office, I sat down to face the mails, which was a little like sitting down to face the music.

There had been a great deal of ballyhoo in recent years about automatic post offices, rocket mail, letter by satellite, facsimile transmissions and similar exploits with a science-fiction flair. Mail had actually been blasted by rocket from a submarine in the Atlantic to the Florida mainland. From there, of course, it proceeded by more conventional means to its destination—taking seven days in all. My predecessor did send a letter from his office in Washington to Newark, New Jersey, via the Echo satellite. The message was beamed by microwave to the satellite which bounced it back to Bell Telephone's space laboratory in Holmdel, New Jersey, which sent it on by wire to the Postmaster's office in Newark where a receiver produced a facsimile. The message: "Shop and mail early"—the annual Christmas appeal.

Some 4½ million dollars had been spent to test high speed transmission of "facsimile" mail by coaxial cable and microwave radio. This futuristic project was announced some months before the Kennedy Administration took office and a pilot operation was set up between Chicago, Washington, and Battle Creek. The first letter was sent just a few days before the 1960 election. The machines which performed this feat would take a sealed letter, open it, scan it and transmit it by microwave to a receiving station which would promptly produce a facsimile of the original letter. Another device would stuff the facsimile into an envelope

38

and address it. This was nothing but another form of telegram
but without rapid delivery at the other end. Transmission took
only a few seconds, of course, but the mailman took considerably
longer. The Post Office is still a walking organization. Each one
of some 100,000 letter carriers walks three thousand miles a year.
In addition, facsimile mail was a blatant intrusion into wire
communication which is a private enterprise.

I thought that such research projects were probing too far into
the distant future, and that the Post Office should concentrate
on projects showing promise of moving the mail more quickly
in the present. I could sympathize with the party who, after
hearing that a study was being made of guided missile delivery
to shoot mail from coast to coast in an hour, muttered that when
that technique was mastered, means of delivering mail from one
side of Washington to the other should be studied.

Accordingly, after January 20, 1961, rocket mail, facsimile
transmission, and related projects were quietly de-emphasized.

But the post office in Providence, Rhode Island, still had to be
faced. And face it I did, very soon after I took office. The Providence post office was the Department's mechanical mailman, its
automated showcase and, unfortunately, its red herring. Critics of
the operation—and there were many—thought that Project
Turnkey, as it was called, might better be dubbed Project Turkey. As far as they were concerned, it was for the birds. Certainly
it had an inauspicious beginning.

The Providence post office was dedicated in a blaze of publicity
on October 20, 1960. The timing of that event, coming as it did
only a couple of weeks before the November elections, seemed to
hint of political considerations. The suspicion was reinforced
when Republican interest in the project waned after the dedication and all but disappeared after the election.

The post office was built and run on contract with Intelex, a
subsidiary of International Telephone and Telegraph. The company had had considerable experience in automating and operating post offices in other countries, but it was the first time in the
United States that the running of a post office was dependent on
an outside concern. The building and all the equipment it con-

tained were provided by Intelex and leased to the Government. Some found this hard to accept. Summerfield said it was cheaper that way. Others, most of them longtime postal employees, found it hard to accept the staff of 70 Intelex men working around the clock in the new post office.

The building itself caused comment. It was a one-story affair and four times larger than the old Providence post office. The theory—very theoretical indeed—was that the new post office would serve all but one county of Rhode Island, as well as the Fall River area of Massachusetts. Residents of the Bay State took a dim view of the whole business, a view which grew considerably dimmer after one man decided to test the new equipment by mailing a letter with a stamp from Czarist Russia. When he learned that his letter had passed unscathed (no mean feat itself) through the Providence postal equipment and into the hands of its addressee, he lost no time in broadcasting the news. The resulting publicity, typical of Project Turnkey, spurred others to the same stunt. Some very unusual stamps eventually entered the United States mails from Providence.

Operations did not begin in the enormous new building until early in December, which meant that the new equipment just had time to break down for the Christmas rush and much of the mail then had to be processed by hand. Employees complained that too few of them had been given the training required to operate the new equipment. Some of those who could operate it complained that the machines were making them ill from nervous strain. You name it, we heard it.

Publicity that swirled about the 16-million-dollar post office had given the impression that it was fully automatic and that mail would henceforth be handled entirely by machine. Only a handful of employees would be needed to push the buttons. However, Project Turnkey had about 1,500 employees shortly after it started. This was 100 more than the old post office had had the previous year and the figures didn't include the 70 men from Intelex. Mail volume increased only slightly, and the new machines began to chew up a considerable part of it, generating more complaints.

All this passed darkly through my mind as I began my ill-starred journey to Providence. I had killed two birds with one stone by inviting the Postal Appropriations Subcommittee to come along. (And that decision was almost to kill a third, the so-called Project Turkey.) Representative J. Vaughan Gary of Virginia and his committee members then decided to visit another of their concerns, the Coast Guard Academy, on the same trip, so the Commandant of the Academy and top Coast Guard brass came along, too. It must have been the uniforms that caused a Providence newspaper to report with surprise that I had brought along an admiral as a military aide.

By the time we arrived at the Providence post office, the entourage had grown to battalion size. There were Congressmen, Coast Guard officers and their aides, reporters, photographers, and television men, postal officials from Washington and Boston and the local office, numerous representatives of Intelex, and a galaxy of lesser stars.

The Postmaster was overwhelmed, as was I, for that matter. Assuming that he would guide us through this mechanical maze, I fell in beside him, the fellow travelers straggling along behind. We strode purposefully the length of the building, which was as big as two football fields, and came up suddenly against a stark, blank wall. The Postmaster had just been following me, he explained. We all laughed—a little nervously.

After it was established that he would lead, we marched over to an elaborate parcel post sorting machine that looked like a gigantic jungle gym high off the floor. Undaunted, the crowd of us—and believe me, it was a crowd—climbed a series of steel ladders to the summit. ("Because it was there," I wanted to say, if someone had asked me why we climbed it.) From our precarious aerie we could have seen the machine at work digesting parcels, if we had dared to look down from that height—and if it had been turned on. So the procession reversed itself and, for some obscure reason, every last one of us left that perch to search for the switch. When it was found and turned on we went back up. By that time we were breathless, and it wasn't due entirely to anticipation—which, as it turned out, was a good thing, because there were no parcels to sort. Not one could be found in the entire post office, and again we made the descent.

After a few more incidents of a similar nature, the Congressmen, thoroughly appalled, went on to the Coast Guard Academy and I departed for Washington. I knew that lunch would not be served on the plane, so I rushed into a restaurant on the way to the airport to pick up a couple of sandwiches in a paper sack. As I sat munching on the plane I saw that I was eating out of a "Beggar Bag" meant for taking scraps home to the dog. It figured.

Back in Washington I waited for the subcommittee to unleash its arsenal. The first salvo came a few days later from Representative Gary. Project Turnkey "failed miserably," he raged to the Washington scribes assembled; its cost to the Government was "grossly excessive"; he and the members of his subcommittee were "thoroughly shocked" at the extent to which Project Turnkey failed to live up to its advance billing.

I was shocked, too, but I didn't believe that withholding payments from Intelex, as the subcommittee ordered, would alleviate the problems. After a time the charges and countercharges diminished in intensity, the furor over Project Turnkey subsided, and we began to do something about it. I encouraged employees at the Providence post office to speak out on their project, to send me their suggestions and criticisms. I met with them to hear what they had to say. I also sent in a task force of postal management experts to beef up morale and efficiency. We were determined to make Project Turnkey work, but we didn't expect it to work miracles.

The problem with Project Turnkey was not so much its failure to live up to its advance billing as that advance billing itself. The project was set up as a postal laboratory in which to experiment with new equipment and new ideas. It was inevitable that some of the equipment and some of the ideas would not work. What made turkey out of Turnkey, however, was that the research program started off with a flurry of glowing press releases which set the pattern that the project was expected to fit. And it was a misfit, that's all.

We kept this experience in mind when we later embarked on postal improvement programs of our own. Before we sent out the flacks to praise our projects, we made sure that the projects would work. This plan of action served us well.

In the fall of 1962 the Post Office started delivering local business mail the same day it was dropped into downtown mail boxes bearing an ABCD (Accelerated Business Collection and Delivery) sticker. We claimed that mail in the box by eleven in the morning would be delivered by three o'clock that afternoon. No newspaperman of conscience could let such a claim go untested, of course. They tried it in Chicago and Wilmington, and the system worked smoothly. But in Washington, where the press has developed a great deal of animal cunning, reporters decided to give us at the Post Office time to relax our vigilance before putting ABCD to the test. Accordingly, when the system was three weeks old, the time was deemed ripe. Reporters fanned out across the city, dropping mail into ABCD boxes at eleven in the morning and returning to their offices to wait. They were confident they'd be waiting until the next morning. But the new system didn't take four hours; in only two and a half all the mail had filtered in. The newsmen graciously conceded defeat. The system had been thoroughly and secretly tested a week before it was unveiled, but we hadn't told reporters that. Simple as ABCD, we said.

Same-day collection and delivery improved mail service in a great many cities, but the greatest operating improvement during my tenure in the Post Office was the ZIP code. The ZIP code system is more important, more extensive, and more promising than any since free delivery started a century ago. You might say that ZIP put zing in the Post Office.

The ballyhoo had been endless, and the talk uninformed about "automating" the mail system, but the need for some improvement was apparent to all. The United States Post Office handles more than half the world's mail—some 70 million pieces each year. This is enough mail to fill a line of railroad cars stretching from Boston to San Francisco. Each year the volume increases by 3 or 4 per cent and there are $1\frac{1}{2}$ million new addresses to serve.

Names, addresses, and the conventional zoning system can no longer efficiently direct this enormous amount of mail to so many different destinations. The human eye must read the address on a piece of mail as many as 8 or 10 times in the course of getting it from sender to addressee. Multiply by 70 billion and that's a lot of eyestrain.

The new ZIP codes actually made it possible to save money and time through using existing punch card and computer equipment in business offices to help in the mail sorting process. Machines can "read" the five-digit code numbers easily. The first numeral indicates one of ten service areas in the country. The second stands for the state or other subdivision within that area, and the third the city. The last two digits are the local postal zone number, or a smaller town post office.

Anybody could see that a machine could comprehend the meaning of 70631 easier than it could locate and direct a letter to Bellefontaine Neighbors, Missouri, or Anaktuvuk Pass, Alaska. Immediately seers prophesied—and bewailed—the end of such American place names as Lost Mule Flat, Deadwood, Painted Post, Wounded Knee, Truth or Consequences, and so on, which were sure to be replaced by the five colorless digits of ZIP. But despite the efforts of Bell Telephone, which was retiring such distinguished exchanges as BUtterfield in favor of 28 in an all-number dialing system; despite the work of the Social Security system in reducing us all to a string of numbers, now showing up on our federal income tax forms; and despite ZIP, the alphabet shows no sign of withering away.

This must have surprised those who foresaw its immediate demise. But the great public interest, or more precisely, the great public furor whipped up by the introduction of ZIP raged no more angrily than the one in 1863, when the Post Office Department came up with another outrageously controversial innovation—addressing mail by street and number. (Before 1863, mail was sent to a name in a city, and each person picked up his own at the local post office.) Counting to ten didn't seem to mellow anybody's ire. Oddly enough, neither did running through the alphabet. But the public controversy had a surprising effect:

when people realized that they weren't going to become anonymous ciphers, they were ready to accept the ZIP code.

The ZIP codes were intended primarily for business mail, which makes up about 75 per cent of first class mail and a much higher percentage of the other three classes. Half the business mail comes from just 25,000 mailers. If those 25,000 firms could be persuaded to use ZIP codes and if the Department could mechanize to a practical extent the 200 post offices which handle 60 per cent of the nation's mail, the results would be far more impressive and far less expensive than those obtained from shooting mail across the country in ICBMs. We believed that there was more potential for the Post Office in IBM.

Accordingly, we proposed a ten-year plan for meaningful, methodical postal mechanization. The plan included installation of more of the "facer-canceller" machines which take unsorted mail, seek out the stamps with an electric eye, position the letter, cancel the stamps and deposit the letter for sorting, at a rate of 500 letters a minute; greater use of ultra-violet scanning devices to recognize and sort out air mail stamps, and machines to sort mail into 600 pigeonholes by means of keyboard signals. It was hoped that major postal users would mechanically pre-sort their mail by ZIP code, and also co-operate with the Post Office in scheduling their large mailings.

In fact ZIP codes began to appear more and more often on the letters of individuals. The public was participating in the plan to a far greater extent than had been predicted. But our department had a considerable way to go before matching the record of West Germany, which for several years has encouraged individuals to use what amounts to a ZIP code. Some 80 per cent of West Germans were participating in the program at the time that our Zoning Improvement Program became effective on the first of July, 1963.

After thorough checking and testing to be sure the system would work, we started off ZIP with zing. Ethel Merman recorded a special version of "Zip-A-Dee Doo-Dah" which was used around the country on thousands of radio and television promotional spots. Hugh O'Brien, television's Wyatt Earp, came down to the Washington Post Office to help beat the drums for ZIP. We had there a life-sized figure of Mr. ZIP himself, who, when pressed, bellowed out the ZIP Song in Miss Merman's voice. We decorated one another with Mr. ZIP lapel buttons, we pasted Mr. ZIP decals on mailbags and mailboxes, and we stuffed the mails with cards explaining the new system. We publicized Miss Merman's participation in our ZIP promotion during her show at the huge Carter Barron outdoor amphitheater in Washington. (I went to the stage during her singing of the ZIP song and offered to play Post Office with her any time.) We promoted ZIP, in short, with all the flair the flacks could muster. And it worked, zippingly.

Chapter 7
NO BUSINESS LIKE
P.O. BUSINESS

DREW PEARSON will testify that a letter bearing no address but "S.O.B., Washington," was delivered to him promptly after he had received a tongue-lashing from President Harry Truman.

The Post Office prides itself on the lengths to which it will go in giving its customers service. In that cause I've acted as mailman myself. One day I was leaving an airplane after having settled my family on board for a flight to Los Angeles when a passenger called out, "Hey, buddy, I forgot to mail these letters. Would you stick them in a mailbox for me?" Old buddy Day did, of course.

In Los Angeles my wife was recounting this incident to a friend while they both stood near one of the windows in a neighborhood postal station. When she had finished a nosy clerk spoke up from behind the window and said dourly, "Mrs. Day, please tell your husband that postal employees are forbidden by the regulations from mailing people's letters for them." I was interested to hear it, but I've not yet been able to find the rule.

Had I found it, I might have invoked this rule in regard to Bruce Alger, the extremely conservative Republican Congressman from Dallas, Texas. One day a large box of stamped, sealed, and addressed envelopes arrived by parcel post addressed to me from New York. A covering letter explained that the letters in those envelopes were soliciting money for Mr. Alger's campaign and asked *me* to mail them so that each would have a Washington postmark. More of the same arrived with another covering letter. I mailed them all, although my better instincts protested.

I'd never expected to be involved in even the smallest way in soliciting funds for Mr. Alger. Indeed, I might have done Mr. Alger a favor if I hadn't bothered. His backers were a little mixed up on that particular mailing. Shortly afterward the newspapers reported that one of his requests for money was addressed to Mr. Democrat himself, my predecessor, Jim Farley.

For most Americans, mail delivery is the most direct and tangible service the government provides, and it is usually a positive, pleasant relationship in contrast to that with the Bureau of Internal Revenue. Nearly everyone likes his letter carrier. The carrier is, in a way, an ambassador of good will from the federal government. The Post Office is the only federal establishment in most towns and villages.

Whatever else it is, the Post Office—because it is not allowed to make a profit—is not a business, but it tries to be businesslike about its operation. Though its postal patrons today pay over 90 per cent of the expenditures of the Post Office, the money it collects goes into the general Treasury. The Post Office can spend only what Congress appropriates to it, which led to a ridiculous contretemps in 1962 when the House failed to appropriate enough money to keep up the existing level of postal service.

Congress had approved a pay raise of nearly 200 million dollars for postal workers. Then the House suggested that the Post Office absorb much of the pay increase! I said if we were to absorb it we might have to eliminate all Saturday mail deliveries and all deliveries to new business and residential buildings less than 90 per cent occupied. The idea of eliminating Saturday deliveries really raised a howl. The Republican leader of the House, Charlie Halleck, accused me of attempting to "blackjack Congress." I pointed out that under the law a Postmaster General who spent more money than Congress appropriated to him was subject to two years in prison, and that I didn't intend to go to jail just to accommodate Mr. Halleck. Eventually some of the necessary money was restored, and Mr. Halleck's mail continued to be delivered on Saturdays, as did everyone else's.

One day while all this was going on, President Kennedy called a meeting of his Cabinet. Because he was involved with the West

German Minister of Defense, the meeting started without the President, who after a few minutes brought his visitor into the Cabinet Room and introduced him. The gentleman made a little speech telling us how impressed he was at seeing with his own eyes this august body pursuing its weighty deliberations.

"Yes," said the President, "they're probably deliberating about how many mail deliveries we're to have."

Not only is the Post Office, under the law, not expected to show a "profit"—it is not expected to break even. For example, the law provides that the users are not expected to pay for the very small post offices (essential to many little towns in their struggle for survival), the losses from charitable, religious, and educational mailings which go at a greatly reduced rate, and the full expense of rural routes, some of which serve only one or two houses a mile.

Making each class of mail pay in proportion to the cost of handling it sounds desirable, but this does not allow for certain social and historic factors that are deemed of great importance. A policy was set in 1958, whereby specified Department costs were allocated to "public service," not chargeable to users. These costs add up to about 10 per cent of what the Department spends. A formula allocates the remaining costs, allowing for such factors as deferred service, preparatory work done by the mailer, and ability to pay.

Members of Congress almost *never* agree that proposals to close or consolidate small post offices have any merit. One cannot always assume these things, however. When a letter arrived from the redoubtable chairman of the Senate Appropriations Sub-committee for the Post Office, Willis Robertson, relating to a proposed consolidation in Virginia, a busy staff man saw the words *Senator* and *consolidation,* and, eager to accommodate, immediately wrote this letter, which went out over my machine-duplicated signature: "Dear Senator: You will be happy to know that we are not going to consolidate the post offices about which you wrote us."

The trouble was that the Senator's two-page letter to me was a forceful demand that the offices *should* be consolidated. I personally hopped over to the Senate Office Building to quiet the explosion which took place when Senator Robertson read what to him seemed like a worse than brusque reply.

In general, I suppose because I approve the philosophy of Oliver Goldsmith's "Deserted Village," I was opposed to the closing of small-town post offices. One I was particularly glad to be able to save, by vetoing a staff decision to close it, was Lily Pons, Maryland. If we let that be wiped off the map it would be no time at all before someone would close the post office at Truth or Consequences, New Mexico. As it is, there are less than half as many independent post offices in the United States today as there were in 1890.

The cent-an-ounce postage rate increase that became effective in January, 1963, was not expected to eliminate the so-called postal deficit, but it did reduce it, of course. Nonetheless, the increase was met by a certain amount of cacophonous squawking.

Before leaving for Japan in April, 1962, to represent the President at the big Osaka International Trade Fair, I had completed testifying before Congressional committees in favor of increasing the postage rate for first class mail. Also, before I left, the pundits were acclaiming the wage settlement just reached between the steel workers and the steel companies as non-inflationary. The steel companies would not raise prices, the learned ones said. (Many people thought the steel companies had said so, too.)

While I was away all hell broke loose. Most of the steel companies announced a price increase of 6 dollars a ton. Even in Japan, some 10,000 miles from the White House, the President's violent reaction opposing the increase came through loud and clear. And there in Osaka, as I read of his opposition, I thought of our proposal to raise postage rates and I could see just what someone was bound to come up with.

Sure enough, before I got back home the President had received a telegram from a man in Colorado which read, "I OBJECT TO $320 A TON INCREASE IN POSTAGE RATES."

"But think what the Post Office provides for the money," I wanted to say. When parcels become unwrapped while passing through the postal system a special group of employees wraps them up again and sends them on their way. The task is somewhat more difficult when the contents fall out, too, but the postal clerks are so conscientious in locating labels for broken parcels that a Catholic priest in San Francisco once received a neatly rewrapped package of women's underwear.

Or consider the episode of the well-traveled Valentine. A letter addressed to a Pittsburgh man whom I had known slightly in law school came to my desk one day for my signature. In the letter I apologized because his Valentine's Day greeting to his son at a prep school in Delaware had finally been returned to Pittsburgh after a journey to England, Greece, and Russia, but not to Delaware.

My curiosity piqued, I leafed through the attachments for his original "Dear Ed" complaint. One sentence of that first letter sent me searching through the files. It read: "How can we expect to win the cold war if our letter carriers can't read the Cyrillic alphabet?" I had never looked at the cold war in quite that light before.

In the files I found memoranda from our headquarters in Washington to a postal inspector in Pittsburgh, from the inspector to the postmaster there, from the postmaster to the superintendent of the tour (shift) during which the envelope had been processed, from the superintendent back to the postmaster, and so back along the channels. It turned out that the envelope was addressed in letters of the Russian alphabet (which seemed rather peculiar on the part of my friend from Pittsburgh, although no cause for nondelivery), but the address was not in the Russian language. Cyrillic letters had merely been substituted for English letters so that the address was meaningless in both Russian and English. But earnest postal people in four countries had tried their best to decipher it—first at our International Mail Division in New York, then in England, Greece, and finally the Soviet Union. When not one of them could figure it out, the letter was returned to the sender in Pittsburgh. And he had the nerve to complain! About my letter of apology? I threw it away.

Postal employees do evince considerable ingenuity, whether deciphering the Cyrillic alphabet or unearthing forgotten towns. For some baffling reason, a company put into the mail in February, 1963, a letter addressed to the purchasing agent of Cowford, Florida, a city which does not exist. In no time at all, however, the letter was delivered to the purchasing agent of Jacksonville. Its name was changed from Cowford in 1822!

After I had made several unsuccessful attempts at tracking down Hopefield, Arkansas, where my grandfather was born in 1837 and which was supposed to be right across the river from Memphis, the Memphis postmaster came to my aid. I hadn't been able to locate it, he explained, because the whole town fell into the Mississippi many years ago.

The alphabet game of ABCD and ZIP was an outward sign of the profound changes that were taking place within and without the world's largest civilian organization—590,000 employees in 45,000 installations reaping each day an astonishing 10½ million dollars in salaries.

The volume of mail was rising, populations were shifting, and the old transportation patterns were crumbling; but the mail still had to be moved, most often in post offices built to the specifications of another day and in accordance with a system that had scarcely changed from the time Benjamin Franklin devised it. ZIP and ABCD, VIM and NIMS and POMSIP were not remedies for tired blood. Despite the jokes (for example, "Old postmen never die, they just lose their ZIP."), they were important factors in pushing the Post Office a little closer to top efficiency.

Decoded, NIMS becomes the Nationwide Improved Mail Service program, aimed at getting big mailers to pre-sort their mail and send it to the post office earlier in the day. As a result of the program, the volume of first class mail dumped on post offices after five o'clock was reduced from 80 per cent of all such mail to about 50 per cent.

In San Francisco we tested vertical conveyors to speed the delivery of mail in high-rise buildings. With their help, in ten minutes one man delivered mail that had once taken several men ninety minutes. We called the system VIM (as yet there is not VIGOR), which stands for Vertical Improved Mail. It will do a great deal to ease the distribution of mail in skyscrapers.

POMSIP (Post Office Management and Service Improvement Program) was a major step in improving the quality of supervision in the mammoth postal system. For years the Post Office has been burdened by favoritism, patronage, and special privileges. Promotion to supervisory and technical jobs in the career postal service often required the support of the local Congressman or, if he were of the wrong political persuasion, of the county chairman. There are only 50,000 such jobs, and competition for them is extremely keen. In many cases, endorsement for a position higher than Grade 4 (where, at a salary around 6,000 dollars a year, most postal employees find themselves for the duration) was graciously given, the only return expected being a modicum of gratitude. In some cases, however, as past scandals have shown, something more tangible was exacted.

But in almost all instances, promotions based on the spoils system exacted a heavy toll in efficiency and morale, and consequently in the rising cost of processing mail. Politically sponsored supervisors sometimes felt they enjoyed a certain immunity from disciplinary measures and performed accordingly. As supervision lagged, the productivity of clerks and carriers dropped, too. As a few persons with the appropriate political support were elevated to high-paying positions, the morale of hundreds and thousands, without that support, sank.

It was my strong belief that good supervision and good employee morale were the greatest needs of the Post Office Department. Accordingly, promotions to supervisory and technical jobs were put on a merit basis (what you know, not whom you know)—to the everlasting horror of those who preferred to dispense jobs like plums to the politically deserving. Essential to the new plan was the so-called "rule of nine," which stated that the man promoted would be one of nine with the highest marks on a competitive examination and would be one of those recommended by a selection board.

Some Democrats, now in control after eight Eisenhower years, reacted to this as violently as the relatives whose rich uncle willed virtually everything to charity. But President Kennedy expressed his approval of my merit promotion plan, even though one of his top staff members resented it bitterly.

The President had, in fact, made it clear to me that he was interested only in improving the efficiency of the postal service, and he gave me a free hand in doing it. I doubt if the Post Office had ever before in its one-hundred-and-seventy-three-year history been allowed to function with so little direction from the White House on matters of *policy*. Matters of politics, as I explained in an earlier chapter, were quite another thing, and the appointing of postmasters and rural letter carriers from outside the career postal service was still a jealously guarded prerogative of the politicians. All this is an anachronism which should be ended. Fortunately, about 40 per cent of the new postmasters appointed while I was in office were career postal people. And no Republican postmasters were removed through phoney investigations, to make room for Democrats.

The new prescription had therapeutic results: for the first time within memory the Post Office ended a fiscal year without adding to the number of its employees. Indeed, when that year ended on June 30, 1963, there were some 24,000 fewer persons working for the Department than had been predicted in 1960. If it had continued to grow at its rate of the recent past, the Department would have had about 70,000 more employees by 1963 than it actually had. Instead, the number of pieces of mail that each man handled went up 12 per cent. Less than 4 times as many persons now handle 16 times as much mail as in 1890, when the Post Office already had 150,000 employees. Most important, it is no longer necessary to hire an additional 10,000 to 15,000 persons each year to cope with the ever increasing volume of mail.

The idea behind VIM and POMSIP and the rest was, of course, to enable the Department to speed delivery of a rapidly increasing quantity of mail without substantially increasing the number of postal employees. Some 90 billion pieces of mail will be riffling through post office slots in 1970. That's about the number of seconds which have ticked by on the clock since 1000 B.C.

The basic pattern of handling mail developed in the years when it consisted, for the most part, of personal letters to and from points along a complete nationwide rail system. There were 10,000 mail-carrying railroad trains in 1920; the number has dwindled to just 1,400 today. The midnight express, snatching mail sacks on the fly, symbolized postal efficiency. The motto was, "The mail must go through"—and it did.

Today, a mere quarter of the post offices in the United States are in cities with rail service. Despite this, the railroads still carry about 60 per cent of all mail, earning a million dollars a day doing it. The Post Office is the transportation industry's biggest customer, spending 675 million dollars each year to transport mail on airlines, trains, trucks, buses, boats, and sixty-six horseback routes, including an eight-mile stretch between Pine Top and Pippa Passes, Kentucky. The last of the Alaskan dogsled mail routes was not replaced by an airplane until June, 1963.

After World War II, the Post Office was confronted with the post-war business boom and population shifts which poured an ever-increasing torrent of mail into a system ill equipped to handle it. (Before the war, the Post Office handled 26 billion pieces of mail; in 1946, 35 billion pieces; in 1963, 70 billion.) The postwar boom was a blessing, but the Post Office sometimes felt that it would "bust" under its burdens. Business was just too good.

Under such circumstances change was inevitable, and inevitably it was opposed. A battle had to be fought to send first class mail by air when fast surface transportation was not immediately available, a system in common use in Europe and Canada. "Airlift" was first started by Mr. Summerfield to compensate for the dwindling number of mail trains. Instead of sitting in the railroad station between the last train out at night—now often an event of the late afternoon—and the first train out in the morning, first class mail would be flown through the night on a nonpriority basis. Railroads, supported by their employee unions, objected violently. Postal employees who sort mail on trains objected, too. Even the airlines, fearing a reduction in airmail which flies at a higher rate, complained. Everyone told his woes to Congress, which is very impressionable in these matters. Consequently, Airlift has had its ups and downs.

Expansion of Airlift was one of three major programs I wanted the Post Office Department to undertake in 1963. The others involved a new approach to the parcel post problem, including a moratorium on excessive rate increases, and gradual elimination of the declining and unnecessary postal savings business. President Kennedy gave me his personal go-ahead on all three programs.

There had to be a long educational campaign and a deaf ear had to be turned to cries of "dictatorship." Such cries arose when the Post Office set down a reasonable minimum size requirement for envelopes because the very small ones were jamming the new postal equipment. As it is, some 700 sizes of envelopes are mailed in the United States on an average day, in contrast to West Germany, where 12 sizes are allowed. In the Soviet Union, where the customer has very little say about anything, only 6 sizes of envelopes are permitted.

Some feared that the abbreviations coined to symbolize improved postal methods spelled only doom for the Department's venerable ways. Others assumed that such efficiency was bound to be costing too much. Take Mr. H. F. Ayres of Shaftsbury, Vermont. He objected that a letter postmarked at four-thirty P.M. on March 14 in New Bedford, Massachusetts, was delivered to his rural address in Shaftsbury at eleven the next morning. Mr. Ayres wrote:

> Overnight from such a distant city to our place in the woods is FANTASTIC.
>
> Such efficiency must cost like the mischief.
>
> And we know of no business or individual who needs such service.

We certainly hope no more money will be spent to keep up
such speed over the roads, let alone spending money to better
the record.

Such a complaint, it must be admitted, was rare, and when it
came it was treasured. What Mr. Ayres found fault with was in
fact the ultimate goal of the Post Office: to deliver 95 per cent of
the mail on the following day to all areas where existing transportation would permit it.

Ordinarily it was not efficiency but lapses from it that drew the
most vociferous complaints. Not all were so good-natured as this
letter from a man in New York City:

Have just finished mailing Easter cards. Used one hundred and
twenty-nine four-cent stamps. On each stamp I had to put
Scotch tape so they would stay on the envelope.

This is not a complaint, but I wonder is there a shortage of
glue for said stamps? Would appreciate your reply in this
matter.

Hope you have a happy Easter.

It was a sticky question, to be sure. But not so embarrassing to
the Post Office as the case of the Smith College acceptance notices. Many girls apply for admission to several leading women's
colleges in the hope of being successful with at least one. When
the colleges sent out their acceptance notices on different dates,
great confusion resulted because applicants would delay final decisions until they had heard from each of the schools to which
they applied. To help solve the problem, seven distinguished
women's colleges in the East, including Smith, painstakingly
worked out a system whereby each school would send out acceptances at exactly the same time on the same day. Then there
would be fewer cancellations, late acceptances, etc.

The system was working beautifully when, a few years ago,
Smith took all its acceptance letters to the post office at the appointed time. In a day or two the inquiries started. Where were
the letters from Smith? Letters from all the other colleges had

been received. The Post Office checked, but found nothing. After days of confusion, frustration, and disappointment, the entire box of letters was found under a counter at the Springfield, Massachusetts, post office. After that, I was rather surprised that Smith admitted my own daughter.

The paragon most frequently urged upon us for emulation was the postal system of the United Kingdom. To suggestions of this sort I used to reply that you get what you pay for. In the United Kingdom, which handles less mail than New York State alone, postal rates are much higher than ours in relation to the cost of living and there are more postal employees in relation to volume, all of which makes possible the much touted two and three deliveries a day to residences. In 1950 the U.S. Congress cut 30 million dollars from the Post Office's appropriation, forcing the end of afternoon mail delivery to homes. The Department has never had the money to resume it. (Nor any real reason to do so, since telephones have become so readily available and so widely used in the United States.)

All told, the United States Post Office has been able to accomplish quite a lot, on sheer ingenuity. Until after World War II it did not even have a research program to cut costs and improve operations on its massive materials-handling job. Now the research budget runs about 12 million dollars a year—although highly vulnerable in epidemics of economizing in Congress—and the Post Office speaks the language of the modern engineer. As I told a group from IBM to prove this point: "For some time we have been installing postal system input buffer devices as temporary information storage units at pseudo-randomly selected locations. Access to these devices—thanks to a major technological breakthrough—has been achieved at a 270-degree rotation from a vertical center line. The control console presents a multi-function control lever to the operator for activating the operational cycle. Maximum extension of the multi-function control lever simultaneously eliminates feedback and permits utilization of the input buffer reset. The feed cycle is subjected to visual scrutiny and is normally served by manual insertion directed by a mixed alphanumeric code. Release of the multi-function control lever automatically transfers the input to the delay-box memory accompanied in many instances by a squeaking signal. Verification is almost always accomplished by a second pull of the multi-function control lever symptomizing an overwhelming post-mailing peak compulsion syndrome."

That describes the ordinary street mailbox. But you've got to speak the language. And so far, fortunately, that still takes people.

Chapter 8
MAN'S BEST FRIEND
HAS TEETH

IN 1818 the stagecoach had just begun to carry mail over the Cumberland Road (now U.S. 40) to and from the West—just the other side of the Appalachians in those days—when the Postmaster General complained that the firm of J. A. Trotter & Bros. was not maintaining its schedule from Greenbrier County to Clarksburg in the West Virginia mountains. Trotter, a direct man, replied, "If the gable end of hell should blow out and shower fire, smoke, and melted lava for forty days and nights, it would not melt the snow on Cheat Mountain so as to get your damned mail out on time."

Conditions are certainly better on Cheat Mountain today, but 100,000 mailmen still encounter some formidable obstacles along their routes. Even in this era of automatic data processors, facer-cancellers, parcel sorters, ZIP codes, and IBM cards popping up everywhere, delivering the mail demands men with stout backs and a willingness to defy snow, sleet, wind, and rain. Yes, and dogs.

Despite the truly astonishing technological advances of the last twenty-five years, man's best friend still has teeth and a mailman's leg still is vulnerable to bite. Some 7,000 mailmen are wounded each year by carniverous canines—not to mention the letter carrier once attacked by a goose and the one hospitalized by a bantam rooster. In 1963, dog bites cost the government a million dollars, chiefly in lost work time and medical expenses. In retaliation the Post Office has tried almost everything but a B-B gun—even cheetah fat, which was recommended by a retired British Army officer living in India. Dogs would stay strictly away from the mailman whose shoes were smeared with the stuff, he claimed. The Department thanked him but explained that cheetah fat was difficult to come by in the United States, as, indeed, were cheetahs. So the Britisher sent along a jar. We smeared it on the shoes of some men in the postal laboratory and called in the dogs. They were not repelled. On the contrary, they slavered enthusiastically over the larded shoes and licked off the cheetah grease with great gusto. Perhaps if they'd been conditioned against cheetahs . . .

That incident reminded us of the letter carrier telling his buddy about the gigantic dog that had taken a tremendous chunk out of his leg. "Gee," said his buddy, "did you put anything on it?"

"No," said the carrier, "he seemed to like it the way it was."

After giving up on cheetah grease, we developed a mixture of mineral oil and hot red pepper packaged in an aerosol spray. We figured that with a little practice a quick-on-the-draw postman could squirt an attacking dog in the face from a range of twelve feet, send the thwarted animal slinking off to the doghouse, and save the postman's shin. Members of the Society for the Prevention of Cruelty to Animals exhibited the degree of horror we hoped the new weapon would arouse amongst the canines. Whereupon the Postmaster of Miami tossed a large salad, dressed it with dog repellent, and ate it. He's probably still simmering, but at least he's alive. Such devotion to the postal system was exceeded in my experience only by a postal employee in Hamburg, Germany, who, in order to inspect a flood-damaged pneumatic mail tube eighteen inches in diameter, had himself pulled through it, carrying a knife and pushing a wire screen ahead of him to ward off rats. Hamburg's system of very large pneumatic tubes might work in a city like New York, which cannot have ABCD service because of the extreme difficulty of getting mail trucks quickly through its clogged streets.

The aerosol spray seems to be working fairly well on the outdoor type of dog, but it doesn't stop the house dog with a propensity to nibble at the mailman's fingers as he pushes letters through the front-door slot. Traditionally, householders with menacing mutts have been put on notice by letter. That approach had two drawbacks; the mailman had to avoid the hostile dog in order to deliver the warning letter, and the dog couldn't read, which I suppose explains why so few of them ever got the message. Now a telephone call from the post office warns the householder that he's in immediate danger of having his mail delivery cut off if his dog isn't tied up.

Dogs will not deter for long the men that weather cannot discourage from their appointed rounds. Consider the young letter carrier in Maryland, his uniform drenched in a cloudburst, who changed to his only other uniform, and was promptly soaked by another downpour. The best solution, as he saw it, was to continue his rounds in bathing trunks and a letter carrier's cap for identification. His particular postmaster saw it differently, when his startled eye fell across the next day's newspaper pictures of the letter carrier so attired, and he suspended the young man whom weather could not stop.

But the Post Office Department headquarters decided to unsuspend him. After all, the motto of the Post Office (derived from the description by Herodotus in the fifth century B.C. of the fleet messengers of Darius the Persian) was:

"Neither snow nor rain nor heat nor gloom of night stays these couriers from the swift completion of their appointed rounds."

These words are carved, a city block long, above the entrance of the General Post Office in New York City. The story goes that many years ago, a rural letter carrier from the midwest, visiting the big city and viewing those words in stone, said to his wife, "Just like those darned bureaucrats. They don't even know how to spell 'carrier'!"

More difficult problems than weather and dogs are the emotions of men. The Post Office is the country's largest employer of Negroes, and it has been notably active in eliminating job discrimination. But emotions run high in this matter, and resolving controversies requires great delicacy. I think of an incident concerning the Negro who delivered mail in my Maryland neighborhood. A householder on his route placed near his front door a small statue of a Negro coach boy in black boots, white pants, red coat, and little cap—why, I don't know, because guests seldom arrive in coach-and-four any more. My letter carrier objected strongly to the figure and asked the householder to remove it. Instead, the patron lodged an angry complaint with the Post Office Department. Someone down the line promptly transferred the carrier to a different route. There was an appeal and a hearing. Finally it was decided that it didn't solve anything to make two mountains out of one molehill and the man was put back in his original assignment. In other words, things were restored to statue quo.

Then there was the time they dropped the beehive at the Post Office. It was an authentic honey factory, buzzing with activity. Beside this one, such postal problems as snarling dogs, hostile elements, and racial storms seemed to lose their sting. When the beehive broke, bees swarmed through the special handling room of the Washington Post Office. A bee specialist eventually rounded them up, with only our pride being stung; someone had to tell the addressee why his hive didn't arrive.

And bees are only one of the live creatures that buzz, flap, and snap through the postal system, striking dread into the hearts of mailmen and, incidentally, doing more to set back postal mechanization than anything since the research budget cut of 1963. Packages containing live scorpions must be labeled "Live Scorpions," and day-old chicks can be mailed only if they can be delivered within seventy-two hours. Pet alligators are mailable if they are securely packaged. Worse still, secure packaging is often ignored by mailers of advertising gimmicks such as sample razor blades. A home repair concern even enclosed a few sample nails in the envelope with every circular it mailed! A nationwide contest conducted by a soft drink company resulted in the mailing of tens of thousands of bottle caps which sabotaged our machines.

Thousands of Americans have discovered when moving that the most economical way to ship books is through the mail in 70-pound lots at the book rate of 6 cents a pound. Low parcel post rates encourage many weird shipments. An entire freight-car load of canned milk was once flown to Point Barrow, Alaska, by parcel post. It had to go by air, because there's no other way to get there.

We were only slightly amused to discover that a Western firm manufactured, for sale at the Seattle World's Fair, picture "post cards" that measured two feet by three feet, the size of an ample desk blotter. As the final effrontery, the card bore the legend, "Postman, do not fold or bend." I could picture a busy letter carrier making his rounds with a few of those signboards tucked under his arm as he attempted to sort mail, collect for postage due, get signatures in insured items, and fend off dogs. After thinking about this for a while, we advised the Seattle people that they could continue to mail the cards, but they'd have to be in crates.

In any enumeration of weird but mailable objects, some of the letters I received should surely be included. A New York advertising man suggested a 5-cent stamp to honor the five senses. "A five-sense stamp," his letter called it, sensibly. Another man recommended that we sell advertising space on the gummed side of postage stamps. He thought that the space, because of its wide though brief exposure, would sell for big prices and clear up the postal deficit. Whenever we received one of the frequent suggestions that we sell advertising on mail trucks, letter boxes and elsewhere, I was reminded of the advertising printed on the toilet paper furnished by the government-owned British Railways.

Many people love to send needling letters to public officials, but the one from veteran reporter Walter Trohan of the Chicago *Tribune* deserves a prize. His letter arrived a couple of weeks after Christmas, 1961. It read:

Congratulations on adding a new dimension to Christmas.
When your predecessor was in office, I used to get all my Christmas cards and packages by Christmas day and it made it quite a burden to get all my "thank you" notes out at one time.
Now, under your administration, here it is two weeks after

Christmas and my cards and packages are still trickling in. This makes it much easier to acknowledge them. Thanks for adding a new dimension to Christmas.

The only way to handle this, I decided, was to reply in kind: "Thank you for your complimentary letter about our Christmas mail service," I wrote. "As one who grew up on the Chicago *Tribune* in Springfield, Illinois, I was particularly flattered to have this praise from such a distinguished source." We had actually had the best Christmas mail service ever that year, and we got along with 75,000 fewer temporary employees than were used during the previous Christmas season.

Every citizen with a complaint about the Post Office wants to take it right to the top. Some years ago *Time* magazine and *Life* magazine were delivered on the same day of the week, instead of being staggered as they are now. An irate lady telephoned the Denver Post Office and, despite all efforts to divert her, insisted on talking to the postmaster himself. When she finally had him on the line, she said crossly: "Mr. Postmaster. My letter carrier is here and he has the *Time* but no *Life.*"

There is the widely told story of the needy little boy who wrote a letter to the Lord. "Dear Lord," he wrote, "Please send me $100." The Post Office routed the letter from one office to another, until, because it obviously required high level attention, it was finally routed to the Postmaster General. He took a 10-dollar bill from his wallet, put it in an official envelope and mailed it to the boy. In a couple of weeks the boy was as penniless as ever. So he wrote another letter to the Lord. "Dear Lord," he wrote, "Please send me another $100. And this time don't send it by way of Washington. They withheld 90 per cent."

Shortly after we announced plans to issue a stamp to honor Dag Hammarskjold, who was tragically killed in a plane crash in the African jungle, a lawyer in Oakland whom I did not know sent me a most surprising letter. In three typed pages after detailing various intrigues involving the Congo, he ended up attacking the proposed stamp: "Don't you realize that when Dag Hammarskjold's body was found in the wreckage, they discovered hidden under his shirt an ace of spades? You ought to be ashamed to be issuing a stamp to honor a man who cheated at cards!"

During various informal chats thereafter I asked Dean Rusk, George Ball, and Adlai Stevenson if they had heard of the ace of spades story. None of them had.

In the Post Office Department, big as it is, the ridiculous rhubarbs have a way of winding up on the Postmaster General's desk along with the major crises. The inverted printings of the Dag Hammarskjold commemorative stamp qualified as a major crisis. The dedicated craftsmen at the Bureau of Engraving and Printing (which is part of the Treasury, not the Post Office) had not let an error of that magnitude slip through for forty-four years when, in 1962, the background color on a few of the stamps was printed upside down. The defective stamps would have brought enormous prices, but I felt that the philatelic aspects of the Post Office Department should be run for the benefit of the small collectors, not as a lottery for the few. Therefore, I ordered the printing of enough additional inverted Hammarskjold stamps to meet the demand. That turned out to be 40 million. A poll among stamp collectors endorsed my action by a narrow margin.

Ordinarily the Post Office does better by those persons, events, or things it commemorates on United States postage. Collectors of postal snafus thought they had another when the stamp issued within minutes after astronaut John Glenn returned from space carried neither his picture nor his name. People assumed that it would honor Glenn, but they were wrong. A statute bans picturing living persons on stamps. Though frequently referred to as the Glenn Stamp, the commemorative was a tribute to the entire Project Mercury–U.S. Man in Space effort. An earlier air hero, Charles Lindbergh, is the only living person ever honored on a commemorative stamp. A 1927 10-cent air mail stamp bore the Lindbergh name but pictured only his plane.

In regard to commemorative stamps, the first step I took as Postmaster General was to reduce their number. The second was to improve their artistic quality. To assist in both these endeavors a Citizens' Stamp Advisory Committee was appointed. Both efforts were successful, although I don't think the Committee was consulted about the "Day $500,000 Commemorative Stamp," which a group from the Post Office gave me for Christmas, 1962—after the Hammarskjold invert incident—and on which my picture was printed upside down.

At the time J. A. Trotter was enduring the hardships of the Cumberland Road, the Post Office hardly felt the need of an employee relations program. Now the postal employees are organized into unions and the question of representation was settled in a referendum while I was Postmaster General.

The postal unions cannot strike, but they have a unique power that other labor unions might well envy. They have power where it counts—with Congress, the Post Office's big boss. Having thousands of local units, including some in each Congressional district, the unions are free to communicate directly with their employers who are also the men their members help elect to Congress. This approach is undeniably effective.

The unions seek to involve Congress in disputes over operating policy, too. They regard work-measurement systems, used to help control costs, as "a detested, dehumanized speed-up," to quote one union man, and Congress has debated the subject for a decade. The Post Office has assured employees that work-measurement data will never be used for disciplinary purposes, but members of Congress are still sponsoring legislation to outlaw the systems.

In March, 1963, I signed for the government the biggest labor agreement ever negotiated. It affected more than 500,000 postal employees, represented by six craft unions in the fifty states. The six unions—each retaining certain exclusive rights at the national level—are the AFL–CIO's Letter Carriers, Postal Clerks, Motor Vehicle Employees and Special Delivery Messengers, the independent Rural Letter Carriers Association, and the Association of Post Office and General Service Maintenance Employees.

The document was the first department-wide contract negotiated under President Kennedy's federal employee labor-management program, which gave official recognition to unions of federal employees. No contract in private industry covered so many persons. But unlike labor contracts in private industry, the postal agreement did not provide higher wages, shorter hours, or increased fringe benefits. These conditions of employment are fixed by Congress and are not subject to negotiation. The contract did cover a wide variety of items from the use of bulletin boards to a new grievance procedure, from vacation schedules to job reassignments. In general, the power of a union behind them makes for a contented group of postal employees, although the employees themselves sometimes cause headaches in the union's upper echelons. Consider this letter from a field representative to the insurance office of one of the postal employee unions:

> Brother William Young Tom changed his name some time ago from William Tom Young. When this change took place Brother William Young Tom requested I inform you of his name change—which I did at once by letter.
> Brother William Young Tom is a very reasonable man, but at times can be quite excitable. When Brother William Young Tom, who used to be William Tom Young, received his new identification card addressed to Young William Tom he became quite excited.
> If we here in Fresno are going to have any peace from Brother William Young Tom, who used to be William Tom Young, but who was never Young William Tom, you must get his name changed and inform him of same. (I wonder why the hell he had to change his name in the first place?)

Every organization has *some* personnel problems, but the Post Office, larger than any, is fortunate in that regard. And so no compliment paid to my administration pleased me more than one from Bill Doherty, speaking as head of the National Association of Letter Carriers. "I don't mean this to sound like a pun," he said, "but for us it's been like coming from darkness into Day."

Some misguided persons seem to look forward to a day when a robot driving a Mailster will clank up to their houses to deliver the mail and perform various related chores. But I don't. Robots could never chat about the weather, and they certainly couldn't replace Marvin Johnson, our letter carrier in Los Angeles. I had been friendly with him long before I had any inkling that I would be entering the postal service. Our friendship continued after I became Postmaster General and moved to Washington, leaving my fourteen-year-old daughter Molly in Los Angeles to finish the school year. On the envelope of a letter to me, she wrote:

> Postman, postman
> Do your duty
> Take this letter
> To my cutie.

When the envelope arrived at my office, it carried another message:

> OK
> It's on its way.
> Marvin.

The only advantage I can see to a robot letter carrier is that it would be impervious to dog bites.

Chapter 9
THE PARTY FAITHFUL

UPON MOVING to Washington we inherited an incredible cleaning woman named Alice from the previous owners of our house. Alice had the tendencies of the cartoon Hazel. On a day off she once telephoned Mrs. Day and asked what she was doing.

"I'm washing my hair," said my wife.

"You can't wash your own hair," Alice said crossly. "This party you're going to tonight is real fancy. Go on out to the beauty parlor."

Thus it was that our cleaning woman provided us with our first simple means of classifying parties in a city whose social life is almost Byzantine in its complexity.

Each year in Washington there are perhaps a thousand or so significant parties. They range from such beauty-parlor affairs as the black-tie dinner and entertainment on the greensward at Mount Vernon (Jackie Kennedy gave it) to a shampoo-it-yourself buffalo meat barbecue at a suburban estate (LBJ was there). Within these extremes spins—perhaps I should say lurches—the Washington party round, dizzily twirling off four or five parties a night for nine months of the year. (Even though the pace of it alone would curl your hair, it keeps plenty of beauty parlors in business.) There is a noticeable tapering off in the long, hot summer when Washingtonians, if they are not actually elsewhere, would like everyone to think that they were.

At a typical reception of moderately large size some 300 persons will show up, hungry enough to eat 25 pounds of shrimp. Local caterers, who have made a big business out of filling these stomachs, estimate that each person will eat ten or twelve bite-sized items and wash them down with three drinks. Multiply by the number of parties per evening, taking into consideration that some of the people will be at two or three of the parties the same evening (the crowd of inveterate party-goers in Washington numbers scarcely more than a thousand), and you've got some hearty intake. Sir Howard Beale, the former Australian Ambassador in Washington, during a farewell toast estimated that in five years on the local party circuit he and Lady Beale consumed 5 beef cattle, 12 sheep, 1,418 chickens, 589 bottles of wine, and 117 bottles of whiskey.

One Washington real-estate firm that wrote to us a few days after announcement of my selection as Postmaster General, apparently thought Mrs. Day and I were going to do more entertaining than anyone who ever joined the government. They wrote that they had just the place we needed for all the big parties we would be giving, a very large house, furnished, "including 109 old fashioned glasses and a poodle sized dog-door." (They forgot to say whether for standard or toy poodle.)

It was surprising to find most people seemed to think anyone in a top federal job was rich. In our case we, in fact, soon developed our own private poverty pocket.

Shortly before I took office, a Los Angeles man whom I had met casually on a couple of occasions sent a telegram inviting me to a party he was giving in Washington. After I accepted, I was startled to discover that literally hundreds of persons, from my fellow appointees to the Kennedy Cabinet to those who swarm on the periphery of politics, were receiving engraved invitations to a huge party in my honor. The invitations were sent out in the name of my Los Angeles acquaintance *and* a Brooklyn Congressman whom I had never heard of. The Washington *Star* was as curious as I as to why this unlikely pair wanted to entertain me so elaborately. Thinking about it for a while, I decided the best thing would be to bow out of the party as discreetly as possible.

A futile gesture, as it happened. The party took place during the great blizzard of Inaugural Eve and I couldn't have gotten to it through the snow even if I'd planned to. Not many others made it, either, and for weeks afterward friends expressed their regrets that the snow had kept them from "my party." Probably the irate hosts and I were the only ones to know I had begged out of it.

Shortly after I took office, a man I had never seen before engaged me in animated conversation at a Washington party. I asked him to identify a gentleman standing at the other end of the room who looked like pictures of the late King Alfonso of Spain that I remembered from my boyhood stamp collection.

"Why, that's the governor of Puerto Rico," I was assured.

A week later, at a diplomatic reception in the White House, the "Governor" explained that he was in fact the Ambassador from Peru and therefore could not enlighten me on the subject of Puerto Rican politics.

To the uninitiated, these incidents may appear to indicate little or nothing about Washington, parties, or politics. But to the party faithful—an ambiguous term which describes those loyal to their political affiliation as well as those who regularly go to everything that serves food and drinks (I use the term here in the latter sense)—these are of a kind with numerous similar incidents taking place in Washington every week. They suggest, for example, what is rarely mentioned outright: at Washington parties many guests may not know their host, nor the host his guests, nor the guests one another—but everybody pretends well. Further, the man who issued the invitations may not be the host at all, if by that one means the person who pays for the party. That guy may not even be invited.

But does that stop the fun? Why, of course not. The circumstances of many Washington parties may be shrouded in mystery and the real reasons for the get-togethers obscure, but everybody's there nonetheless, spearing shrimp, sipping Scotch, and of course trading tidbits of information—gossiping, if you will. Before they succumb to party fatigue, Washington's intrepid party-goers trade on rumors, perhaps because many of them are lobbyists, wheeler-dealers, and writers of trade journals, privately circulated letters, and newspaper columns. Peddling off one piece of "inside" information in exchange for another is the business parties are all about, and, as everyone knows, the real reason for a Washington party is the transaction of business.

Sometimes this verges on the ridiculous. At one dinner a lady I didn't know insisted on telling me in grim and tiresome detail about her series of mishaps in trying to mail a package from the Washington Post Office. After she had gone on and on, I suggested that the next time she wanted to mail a package she should phone me and I would hustle down to the Post Office, get behind the counter, and handle the transaction personally. I wonder if a guest at a dinner party would complain to the head of American Telephone and Telegraph that he's lost a dime in a pay phone. The volume of the two operations—postal and telephonic—is roughly the same.

Many people outside Washington thought it strange that at a White House ceremony in the summer of 1963 Senator Goldwater chatted warmly with President Kennedy. However, 1963 was not an election year. Then, too, strident attacks in political speeches do not usually arise from personal animosity, although after a while they may engender some. Lastly, if a politician does feel a personal animus toward another, he does his best to veil it. People at social gatherings in Washington generally take a more broad-minded attitude toward political differences than people in Los Angeles, or than the crowd in the locker rooms of suburban country clubs elsewhere in the country.

I remember once being introduced as a dedicated Democrat to a man in Chicago who commented, with no intention of humor, "I admire your courage more than your judgment." Although people may think like this in Washington, they rarely say so. The attitude expressed by a prominent Los Angeles business executive—"Any businessman who is a Democrat is a Mongolian idiot"—is more prevalent in California than in Washington. Democrats and Republicans mingle happily in Washington without the verbal sparring that political differences cause in less urbane cities.

Kenneth Galbraith, highly readable economist and long-time friend of the Kennedys, tells this story on himself. One day while he was visiting at the White House, the President said: "Jackie is

quite annoyed that we have been here in the White House over
two years and not once has she been out to lunch at a Washington restaurant. Ken, you are homely enough for me to trust. I
want you to take her."

Galbraith, who had just returned from being Ambassador to
India, promptly obliged. Having heard that the Jockey Club Restaurant at the Fairfax Hotel was decidedly "in," although he had
never been there, he phoned for a lunch reservation for two for
the following day, not mentioning who his companion would be.

"Being a rustic-looking six foot six," Galbraith recounts, "I
have always found that headwaiters at plush restaurants give me
the once over and promptly consign me to a little table crowded
back by the men's washroom where the door bangs against my
protruding knees. I saw that same look coming onto the face of
the headwaiter when I arrived at the Jockey Club with Mrs.
Kennedy half hidden by my gangling frame. Suddenly the headwaiter saw her, went into a frenzy of oozing hospitality and
steered us to the best table in the place.

"That evening as it happened, I had plans to take the Arthur
Schlesingers to dinner and, having learned of this very good
restaurant, I went there again with no reservation. The same
headwaiter was at the door and when he spotted me he beamed
unctuously: 'Your *usual* table, Mr. Galbraith?' "

Another Washington restaurant, Paul Youngs, became "in"
because Joseph P. Kennedy chose it as the location for a supper
dance at which the President-elect and his family, official and
otherwise, enjoyed themselves until four A.M. the early morning
of Inauguration Day. Mary Louise and I, not having such incredible vitality, decided to leave at the conservative hour of two A.M.
and we offered to drive Senator and Mrs. John McClellan home
through the raging blizzard outside. The drawback to this
thoughtful gesture was that our driver and the car containing our
two daughters and son were no place to be found. After leading
the distinguished Senator on a futile exploration trip through
drifts over his knees, I finally happened upon a car just being
vacated by a friend from Los Angeles. We four climbed aboard
and made it to our hotels. After some calls to police headquarters

and with the diligent help of the Secret Service, it was four-thirty A.M. before we retrieved car, driver, and children.

At the center of the social merry-go-round are White House entertainments (the complete guest list and menu are always published in the Washington papers). Clustered around the center are private dinners of an official or semi-official nature, the kind of parties that Alice would describe as "real fancy," requiring something more than a home permanent. These are the command performances of social life in Washington, and some of the performances are entertaining indeed.

What thoughts, planning, and preparation go through the mind of a new Cabinet wife when a White House invitation is received. Usually arriving by mail with the beautiful stamp of the President's house and the American flag flying above, the invitation comes three weeks prior to the event. It is handsomely engraved with the name of the invitee inserted by hand in matching script. The invitation is answered promptly and formally on plain white stationery, perhaps with the "Green Book" as a guide and crutch until the proper wording has become familiar: "has the honor to accept" instead of "accepts with pleasure."

However, White House social events do not always proceed with such proper orderliness. One mid-afternoon a rush telephone call invited us to a reception President Kennedy was giving *that evening* for a large group of out of town newspaper publishers and their wives. I already had scheduled for that evening a speech at a hotel to a visiting high school delegation from Illinois and a departure by train with my son and two other officials and their sons for a quick fishing trip in South Carolina. My wife had only a half-hour notice of the reception by the time my secretary tracked her down. In that time she managed to change her dress, pack our son's suitcase, pick him up at school, and rush to meet me at the hotel where I was making the speech. After we arrived at the reception other Cabinet wives told us of their frenzied moments responding to the last-minute call. One left a newly arrived house guest at home to fix her own dinner. Another's dog got sick just as she was rushing out the door and her husband was delayed outside in the limousine while she did some strenuous carpet scrubbing on her hands and knees. But there was a good turnout of the Cabinet and their wives for only three hours' notice and we helped to deflect some of the publishers who were crowded around the President like a swarm of bees, each no doubt telling him in a few well-chosen sentences just how the country should be run.

When dinner was announced at the white-tie affair the President of Peru gave for President Kennedy at the Embassy in Washington, I was engrossed in conversation with the President. As we moved toward the dining room, my garter broke and dangled from my trousers, dragging across the floor. Without missing a step, or a point, I shifted to a rapid hop on one leg, and removed the garter from the other. My wife, who had witnessed the spectacle from across the room, later said that it was a remarkable performance.

The conversation in which I was so interested concerned the large number of empty seats at the joint sessions of Congress sometimes convened to hear a visiting head of state. I had noticed it on several previous occasions, but it was particularly apparent earlier that day when the President of Peru addressed the Congress. Many Senators and Representatives neither were present nor had arranged for staff members to fill their seats.

The problem is now being avoided more than corrected. There are now more than 120 independent countries, and the leaders of most of them find a much ballyhooed state visit to Washington can do a lot for personal prestige, particularly if their positions are not too secure. As a result of the increase in state visits, the standard program has had to be curtailed. Very few visitors address joint sessions any more, two-day visits are more general than three, and visitors arrive by helicopter on the South Lawn of the White House to save the President a trip to the airport. Instead of the long ceremonial drive from the airport back to Blair House (across the street from his own quarters, where the President puts up his guests), there is now on occasion a short, manufactured parade through the streets near the White House.

After all the elaborate and expensive preparations, state visits seldom produce much of substance. Often the head of state isn't in office long afterward (President Prado of Peru, for example).

Sometimes he turns out to be a transitory friend. When President Ayub Khan of Pakistan arrived, Washington went all-out to give him a red carpet welcome that included a joint session of Congress, at which he told the assembled lawmakers, "Give me foreign aid if you know what's good for you," or words almost that blunt. President and Mrs. Kennedy arranged a splendid, waterborne procession down the Potomac to Mount Vernon, where an elaborate dinner awaited him. There were other festivities of a similar grandeur. By the summer of 1963, however, Ayub was mad at us because of our aid to India, his enemy in the Kashmir dispute. To spite us—or to blackmail us—he was even making overtures to Communist China.

The mechanics of state luncheons and dinners are extremely intricate. Several days in advance of the event, each invited American official receives a guest list complete with the proper title of each person and a set of biographies of the visiting chief of state and his retinue of officials.

When the American guests arrive at the White House they are told by one of the numerous young military aides where to stand in the East Room in order to be in proper protocol order. During the wait there may be a cocktail (a change from Eisenhower days). At the appointed time the Marine Band strikes up a fanfare and the President and his wife and the state visitors enter through the center doorway. The guests file by shaking hands and proceed directly to their places at table.

Even in that elegant setting and with highly experienced staff there are the same slip-ups which plague the do-it-yourself hostess. At our first formal state dinner at the White House, the fireplace in the State Dining Room smoked stubbornly despite frenzied efforts of several attendants, and a waiter spilled a pitcher of cream on a Dallas department store owner at the table where I was sitting. Also at that table was Dr. Spock, the expert on raising children. He, like many non-government guests at White House dinners, was flattered to be invited but had no idea why he was.

If an American is seated next to a foreign visitor who does not speak English, an interpreter is seated between but slightly behind them, where he can hear what is said and translate it, but not where he can eat. This is a little unnerving at first, but by the time the meal is over one has become accustomed to it. The state luncheons present a problem of their own. After six or seven courses, four kinds of wine, a toast and a response to the toast, the meal may well last until three o'clock, leaving the distinguished visitor barely time to prepare to face a similar gastronomic extravaganza in the evening.

At the state luncheon for the King of Morocco, the King conversed through an interpreter with the Secretary of State, Dean Rusk, and his after-luncheon toast was in Arabic. American guests seemed to shy away from the King in the few minutes afterward when the gathering was breaking up, fearing, I suppose, that Arabic was all he understood. I found, however, that he spoke easy idiomatic English. When speaking more or less officially, many visitors prefer to use their native tongue, and not for entirely chauvinistic reasons. Usually they can be more precise in their first language, and precision is important in international affairs.

Official dining abroad isn't any simpler. I found the numerous confrontations with elaborate meals the most unnerving part of my few official trips to foreign countries. In May, 1963, I went to Paris for the truly splendid centennial celebration of the first International Postal Conference—three days of elaborate entertaining and ceremonies. I had been chosen to speak at the opening session because my predecessor of one hundred years before, Montgomery Blair, thought up the whole idea of international cooperation on postal matters.

Montgomery Blair, Abraham Lincoln's Postmaster General, started city mail delivery service and the postal money order system, even with the Civil War going on. He is also credited with erasing during his tenure the Post Office Department's deficit, although the Department always operates in the black in war times and did so even during World War II. But his magnificent idea of international co-operation gave birth to the Universal Postal Union, the oldest and perhaps most successful world organization of governments.

When I arrived in Paris for the conference I found an invitation waiting to a luncheon a couple of days later at the home of the American Ambassador, Charles Bohlen. The next day, as I entered the conference hall to make my speech, I noticed a vaguely familiar face behind the Costa Rica sign in the front row of desks. Inasmuch as I had met in Miami only a few weeks previously with the heads of the Post Office Departments of the Central American Republics, I assumed that I had met the gentleman there. So I said to him, "Glad to see you again."

He was equally cordial, and said, "I'm looking forward to seeing you at lunch at the Embassy on Thursday."

"Oh, are you going to the Embassy?" I asked with some surprise.

"I *am* the Embassy," he retorted, as I realized too late that he was Chip Bohlen, the Ambassador.

When Thursday arrived and we went to the Embassy, I tried to apologize for my blunder, but Bohlen was more concerned with withdrawal symptoms from cigarettes, after thirty years as a chain smoker. To help him over the jitters he "smoked" a plastic cigarette as he talked. So did his loyal second in command, Mr. Lyons, who had also given up smoking tobacco for chewing on plastic.

The luncheon at the Embassy was memorable for another of those ludicrous incidents that sometimes enliven official entertaining: the Assistant Postmaster General for Facilities ripped his pants. Actually, to say Sid Bishop's pants ripped is a major understatement; the fact is, the seat gave way completely. When standing, Bishop lurked with his hands discreetly behind him. Luncheon, being seated, was simple. Then, when he was going down the stairs to leave, our Chief Postal Inspector, Henry Montague, followed closely behind to cover up the disaster area, and the situation—but not the pants—was salvaged.

So many big ceremonies are handled so clumsily that I have sometimes felt that there should be a Czar of Public Events in Washington. When John Glenn paraded from the White House to the Capitol after his triumphal return to Washington from outer space, the sidewalk spectators who stood in the pouring rain to watch him saw nothing but the two big television trucks that hugged close on each side of the Glenn car.

And there is no telling how many people were in a rage as they left one of the fanciest late evening receptions that Washington had seen in many years. They were fortunate, however, that their evening clothes weren't in tatters. The occasion was the opening of the Mona Lisa exhibition at the National Gallery of Art. All the Senators and Representatives and their wives, and hundreds of other people, including the press, received invitations to the black-tie affair. President Kennedy and André Malraux presided, but only a handful of the huge crowd that came could see or hear, because the public address system broke down. In the mob scene, the President's mother, Rose Kennedy, was discovered sitting on a bench far away from the focus of attention. Even she had given up, probably before seeing the picture—a nearly impossible feat at that fiasco.

Notwithstanding the difficulties, the frustrations, the expense, and the chaos such formidable entertaining engenders, parties continue apace, from state dinners, balls, private dinners, and receptions to the massive events that are more or less public— "freebies," in the argot—at which the hungry feed and the thirsty drink, just so long as their dress is decent and their actions reasonably civilized, and the provisions at buffet and bar hold out. One who follows the freebies faithfully is soon a familiar face, and is "in" with invitations.

No talk of Washington parties is complete without some mention of Washington hostesses. There is Perle Mesta, "Two-Party Perle," as she is sometimes called in reference to her temporary switch in allegiance from Democratic to Republican parties when Johnson did not receive the Democratic Presidential nomination in 1960. Her disappointment was so great, she said, that she turned to Nixon. There is Gwen Cafritz, who gives two major parties a year, one at Easter and one in the fall for the opening of the Supreme Court. Mrs. Robert McCormick, widow of the publisher of the Chicago *Tribune,* is a prominent Republican party-giver. When my wife and I arrived at one of her parties, she explained to some of her guests that she wanted to have at least one Democrat in attendance. Another Washington hostess, Frances Parkinson Keyes, is far better known as America's most widely read novelist. Mrs. Keyes, the widow of a United States

Senator from New Hampshire, invited us to several dinner parties because I was the "novelist" in the Administration.

Regardless of their differences in taste and style, Washington
hostesses have one common concern—protocol. The rules of protocol—who sits next to whom, who is introduced to whom, who
leaves before whom, who stands for whom, and so on—are complex, but they are also a convenient means of avoiding injured
pride, both personal and, in the case of diplomatic relations,
national.

One night after dinner at an Embassy I found myself next to
an extremely protocol-conscious Washington lady. She talked a
great deal about the rules and formalities and such other matters
that interested me very little. The lady didn't like my politics and
I think she felt I needed to be enlightened about how things are
properly done in the world of people who really count.

I was the second-ranking guest at that particular party. The
first was an important Ambassador who quite frequently gets so
carried away with good conversation that he forgets the time.
None of us was supposed to leave until he did, which he showed
no signs of doing. The protocol-minded lady became more and
more impatient to leave and as the evening wore on she was
faced with a real dilemma. Finally, she could stand it no longer
and turned to me crossly and said: "I assume you have to get up
early and do some work tomorrow. An Ambassador doesn't ever
have to worry about getting up. Tell the hostess you have to go
so we can leave."

Although the rules of protocol were designed to prevent
affronts, injured dignity and such, they are not always successful.
One night at a huge banquet in the Sheraton Park Hotel the two
tiers of speakers' tables were labeled Upper Deck and Lower
Deck. One Congressman was very incensed because his colleague,
prominent in legislation for the military, was seated at the Lower
Deck.

"Lower Deck, indeed," he complained to me. "If it weren't for
him we wouldn't even have a Navy, let alone decks."

Another incident involved Sargent Shriver, President Kennedy's brother-in-law and the director of the Peace Corps. His
hostess at a buffet-dinner party repeatedly addressed him by his

first name and, after a time, another guest, a retired general, seemed noticeably grumpy. The hostess asked him what was wrong.

"You gave that enlisted man the best piece of roast beef," he said.

Chapter 10
"HE'S A
DEMOCRAT"

AT THE TIME everyone was following the events of General Douglas MacArthur's memorable run-in with President Truman over the conduct of the Korean War, Leroy Lincoln, president of Metropolitan Life Insurance Company, came to Chicago to speak at an Executives' Club luncheon. He made a typical speech intended to appeal to an audience of businessmen he assumed were all Republicans. He succeeded smashingly, especially with the line, "Old Democrats never die. They just smell that way."

I was Insurance Commissioner of Illinois at that time, a peppery, hard-hitting young official in Governor Adlai Stevenson's administration, and I was grievously offended, particularly so, I suppose, because I was very deeply committed to the Stevenson-for-President movement that was then beginning. After returning to my office from the luncheon I sent off a stuffy letter to Lincoln objecting to his crack about Democrats.

Lincoln had the perfect rejoinder. He sent me a photostat of a note from Harry Truman. "Dear Roy," it read. "Someone passed on to me your quip about old Democrats. I got a big laugh out of it. It's great." Lincoln added this note to me: "If Harry Truman can think it is funny, so can you." I was forced to agree, and as time went on I began to see more and more humor in this political business.

At a cocktail party in Los Angeles I was very much amused by my conversation with a major business mogul. According to him he was a strongly *nonpartisan* advocate of better government. "What we should have to get better officeholders," he said, "is greater rank and file interest in government. People of modest incomes should contribute to political campaigns. Why, factories and offices should let employees have political contributions deducted from payroll checks, just as is done with group insurance and Community Chest," he said, warming up to his nonpartisan plan.

"That's a good idea," I agreed. "One big company in California already did it, before the last election."

"How did it come out?" he asked.

"The Republicans got 35 per cent of the money and the Democrats 65 per cent."

"Well, *that* idea's no good," he said, with finality.

A story that goes around the Prudential Insurance Company concerns one of its executive vice presidents who, when asked to run for United States Senator from New Jersey, instantly replied, "No, I don't want to leave the Prudential. I like politics too much." Politics aside, my past experience with the Prudential was almost ideal training for the Post Office. I doubt if any other private organization has so many parallels to the postal establishment as a giant life insurance company. Both have huge numbers of employees and offices in every city. Both handle large sums of money and concentrate on good service and good will. Prudential, like the Post Office, is divided into regions for decentralized management, and, like the Post Office, has an Inspection Service to see that none of its money goes astray. Both have the same supervisory hierarchy, levels of salary classification, and union organizations. Both the Prudential and the Post Office involve endless meetings, conventions, and travel for their executives.

When I was with the Prudential, its national political tone was not exactly that of the Americans for Democratic Action. Like many businesses, it was conservative and pretty much Republican, but the company and its employees were far more tolerant of different shades of opinion that a certain neighbor of mine in Los Angeles.

After I was appointed to the Post Office, FBI agents began interviewing all sorts of people as to whether I was a respectable citizen. I suppose they talked to sixty or seventy business associ-

ates, friends, neighbors, and former neighbors. The lady next
door had never been too friendly, since she disapproved of our
politics. To the FBI man who called on her, she said haughtily:
"I have only a nodding acquaintance with Mr. Day. But I can tell
you *one thing* you ought to know about him." She lowered her
voice and the FBI man leaned closer. "He's a Democrat!"

I'm sure that, to her, was the ultimate in damnation.

I passed the security check anyway. Shortly afterward the diligent agents of the FBI came around to interview me about another man being considered for a Federal appointment. His name
was Adlai Stevenson. "He's a Democrat," I said. Adlai passed,
too.

A conservative group, our Los Angeles neighbors. A couple of
years before, one of them had asked my wife to join some other
women for coffee and "to hear the Welch records." She thought
they would be Joseph Welch, the pixie of the televised McCarthy
hearings. That evening, Mary Louise told me about the records.
On them a man named Welch accused Secretary of State Chris-
tian Herter of being pro-Communist, said that other public officials were dupes of the Communists, and much, much more. At
that time neither of us knew anything of Robert Welch or the
John Birch Society, but I had heard of other extremist groups
that involved people without their ever knowing it. So I asked
my wife if she signed anything at the coffee. "Well, I did put my
name in a guest book," she said. She called the woman up and
told her to take her name off the guest book.

Two years later when some of the members of the neighborhood association wanted to give a good-bye party for us, the
people who had been at that coffee session vetoed the idea because we had refused to join their chapter of the John Birch
Society.

It took me a while, but eventually I began to see humor in such
antics. I also grew to pity the people involved. They are the kind
who are fearful of the foreign born, of labor unions, of intellec-
tuals, and of the rank and file of ordinary people. They believe,
I'm sure, that all the unemployed are lazy and that all the small
farmers should give up and leave their farms. They tend to see all

sorts of devils in the strangest places—even, I might say, in the person of the Postmaster General.

I think the man who invited me to talk before the annual dinner of the Los Angeles YMCA, of which I was a director and vice president, felt much the same way about Democrats as my Los Angeles neighbor. After seeing an advance text of my speech, he called me in Washington in a state of great excitement.

"Your speech is too political," he said.

"What on earth is political about it?" I asked. It was a standard patriotic speech about youth, referring in passing to the importance of certain public issues which would affect youth in the future.

"You mention the President's trade bill and metropolitan area government," said the outraged chairman of the Los Angeles YMCA. "I suggest that when you arrive here we get together and rework the speech."

"Rework it nothing," I said, a little outraged myself at that point. "I have a lot of other things to do in Los Angeles. Just throw the speech in the wastebasket and I'll make an eighth-grade graduation exercise speech such as you apparently want." And I did.

I also had a few little run-ins with the Birchers while I was Postmaster General. Most of them were over the slogan they wanted to use on their postal meters. "This is a Republic, not a Democracy. Let's keep it that way." They didn't like it either when I pointed out that both the Soviet Union and Red China used the word "Republic" in the official names of their governments.

Such minor nuisances aside, my job was the third best in Washington. The two better ones are held by the United States Senators from Nevada. They have only about 400,000 constituents, who are 2,500 miles and three time zones away. When the Senators arrive at their offices on Capitol Hill, Nevada voters are still in bed. By the time they might telephone Washington, the Senators are out to lunch. When the Senators return, their Nevada constituents have gone to lunch. When the constituents return from lunch, the Senators have gone home. Actually Senators Bible and Cannon are very hard-working men. If Nevada can't get something done by relying on the Bible it can use a Cannon.

The elected representatives of the nation every so often sally forth to refresh themselves at the wellsprings of power. To put it baldly, they go home to round up votes in order to come back to Washington for another two- or six-year term. Former Governor (now Senator) Gaylord Nelson tells of giving a try to a vote-seeking technique which was not really his style. He greeted a small-town Wisconsin store owner, a complete stranger, with a big smile and handshake.

"I'm Governor Nelson. Haven't I met you some place before?" he said.

"I don't know," replied the man. "I meet so many people I can't remember them all."

Such are the dangers of life on the hustings.

Once elections are safely past, things can be different. Witness Stephen Young, the outspoken Senator from Ohio. After Mrs. Kennedy's trip to India and Pakistan one of his constituents wrote him:

> I read in the paper that the horse which was given to Mrs. Kennedy in Pakistan was shipped to the United States on an Army transport. I have several horses which I would like to get shipped to various places overseas. Please send me a schedule of Army transports so that I can get my horses shipped free.

The Senator replied:

> I have your letter in which you insult the wife of the President.
>
> I don't see what you need with a horse (at your address) when there is already a jackass there.

When he wrote that letter, Senator Young did not intend to run again. He later changed his mind and was re-elected!

The late Speaker of the House, Sam Rayburn, ran for election again and again, but he was no more tolerant of a stupid letter from a constituent than was Senator Young. The Speaker had a standard reply:

Dear Sir:

Some crackpot sent me a letter and signed your name to it. I knew you would want to know right away so that you can take proper action.

One day a Senator with a reputation as a character was delivering a speech from a prepared text—prepared by someone else—that he had not read before. After gesturing his way through one long, oratorical paragraph, he stopped abruptly, looked at the text again, and blurted, "I don't agree with that at all." Postmaster General Jim Farley had an aide called, by all and sundry, Senator Lyons. According to rumor he had once been a member of the Colorado State Senate. Since the only discernible duty of Senator Lyons consisted of keeping his boss's scrapbook, he was known within the Post Office Department as the Pastemaster General. (The position no longer exists.)

Political "characters" are of course distinct from the authentic political wits, one of the greatest of whom is Adlai Stevenson, whose veto messages as Governor of Illinois were sometimes classics. In 1949 the Illinois Legislature passed the "Cat Bill" which provided that every cat, when off its owner's premises, had to be on a leash! The bill bore the impressive title: "An Act to provide Protection to Insectivorous Birds by Restraining Cats." In vetoing it Stevenson wrote:

The problem of cat versus bird is as old as time. If we attempt to resolve it by legislation, who knows but what we may be called upon to take sides as well in the age-old problems of dog versus cat, bird versus bird, even bird versus worm. In my opinion, the State of Illinois and its local governing bodies already have enough to do without trying to control feline delinquency.

Posterity was no doubt deprived of a memorable veto message when the bill introduced by State Senator (later United States Congressman) Roland Libonati did not pass the Illinois House. The bill would have required a cuspidor in every room of every

public building in Illinois except schoolhouses. After the proposal
passed the Senate I wrote a poem about it:

> A bill has passed the Senate
> About which some are skeptical,
> Which would give a legal mandate
> To a rather crude receptacle.
> For those among the public
> Who may not approve of this,
> We point out that good government
> Should not be hit or miss.
> We recommend approval
> For Libonati's legislation.
> We trust that it will live up
> To our best expectoration.

By failing to pass the bill, the Illinois House denied Adlai equal
opportunity for a proper comment.

Johnson Kanady, the Chicago *Tribune*'s reporter covering the
state government in Springfield in those years, spent a great deal
of time trying to discover the mainspring of Adlai's wit, which
was particularly ebullient at his press conferences. Finally Kanady
decided that Adlai's aides learned in advance of the conference
the questions that would be asked. Then they would put their
heads together with Stevenson to contrive a lot of witty replies.
Kanady wove this rather improbable theory into a story that appeared in his newspaper. The story spurred me again to verse:

> You can buy at the A&P store if you try
> Fresh potatoes all peeled and ready to fry,
> And biscuit or cake dough already mixed
> And a tasty sage dressing that's right there all fixed;
> There is cheese that is sliced, and juice that is squeezed
> And all kinds of items by which labor is eased.
> You might think these achievements were quite a sensation
> When it came to the art of advance preparation;
> But again we discover that new trails have been blazed
> By our Governor who hates all ineptness and waste.

> The Trib has detected, we know not from what clue,
> A State institution that must be quite new;
> It turns out that press sessions are pre-fab with glee
> Produced by the efforts of G.P.W.D.*

Kanady thereupon "exposed" the horrendous tact that a history of Stevenson's record as governor of Illinois, which I had written as source material for the press flocking around the state capital in 1952, had actually been reproduced on state-owned mimeograph paper!

Illinois seems to be a hazardous place for a politician, or even a nonpolitical Postmaster General. It was there I discovered at the last minute that on a late-night television program on which I was scheduled, another panel member was to be Malcolm X, then second in command of the Negro-nationalist Black Muslims. I did not want to be forced into arguing politics, or anything else, with such a controversial figure, particularly since the Post Office has 100,000 Negro employees. (Months later, the Civil Service Commission ordered several probationary Federal employees fired because they stated that in the event of war they owed their loyalty to Black Muslim Islam, not to the United States.) So I said that I couldn't appear on the program if I were to be teamed up with Malcolm X. This particular show consists of a group of people sitting around a table, drinking coffee and talking from midnight to three in the morning. I went on in the early part of the program, with a group that included an English nobleman who wanted to renounce his title in order to serve in the House of Commons. Malcolm X, who joined the circle after I was back at my hotel watching on television, said many ridiculous, inflammatory things in an ultra-polite, almost unctuous manner. He addressed all the men as "sir" once or twice in every sentence, including the Englishman who wanted to put aside his title. The Englishman finally blurted out, *"Please* stop calling me *sir.* I have a *thing* about that."

Malcolm X was mystified. He had missed the introductions in which the Englishman's predicament was explained.

(* Governor's PRE-pared Witticism Division)

In politics there are ordinarily so many debatable issues and so many occasions for dispute that it just isn't practical to carry grudges, but there are, of course, exceptions. There was one such exception in my case. It followed a tantrum that a prominent Senator threw in my office because I didn't agree with him on the location of a regional post office. I didn't mind the tantrum but I did mind the Senator saying that if he didn't get his way he would "attack President Kennedy on Cuba," which he promptly proceeded to do. The Senator and I had avoided each other for nearly two years, when suddenly we found ourselves seated next to one another at a speaker's table. Since I was not aware of the seating arrangements in advance, I couldn't avoid that occasion as I had avoided the meeting with Malcolm X. The Senator and I tacitly decided to overlook our last regrettable meeting, and we chatted most amiably through luncheon. But our new chumminess was soon subjected to a severe strain. Also on the program was Drew Pearson, who, seeing the Senator and me so friendly, decided to recount to the audience the blow-by-blow story of the regional office—Cuba and all. Miraculously, the Senator and I have remained friends.

Avoiding one's political enemies isn't really as tricky as escaping the stigma of one's political friends. When Abraham Ribicoff resigned as Secretary of Health, Education and Welfare to run for the Senate, there was a party for him on the Secretary of the Navy's yacht, *Sequoia*. After dinner, Abe made a little speech in which he said it had been difficult for him to maintain the image of a moderate Democrat in the campaign at home in Connecticut because he was always being associated, in the minds of his constituents, with such administration "super liberals" as Orville Freeman, Arthur Goldberg, and Walter Heller. Bob Kennedy broke in with a quick reply: "Tell your people back home the President never has any Cabinet meetings and you've never even *met* any of those fellows."

As for me, when I was with the Prudential, many people wondered how a person with my progressive political views had managed to become a senior officer in a conservative company. Later, some of the same people wondered how a person with my moderate political views could be a Cabinet member in a Democratic Administration.

Of course there are some people in the Democratic Party to whom fiscal responsibility is only a tiresome cliché, but these people confuse what is desirable with what is feasible. They want a full-fledged New Deal every couple of years. They want every public program to be handled and paid for from Washington. I have always believed that it is essential to have a dynamic and successful business community in order to protect our free economy and to provide the tax base for supporting our great Federal programs. But the business community does not respond dynamically to fiscal irresponsibility. I believe that President Kennedy was in tune with the times in his efforts to co-operate with business and to exercise restraint in economic policies. But then, I'm from the moderate wing of the Democratic Party, an organization broad enough to accommodate—sometimes a bit uncomfortably, it is true—Frank Lausche as well as Hubert Humphrey, and even Harry Byrd. All of them I consider my friends and of course, as I said more than once when questioned as Postmaster General about my stand on various Administration programs, I always stand steadfastly with my friends.

One Administration proposal to which I remained opposed, however, was the program of medical care for the aged. I was convinced it would eventually end up raising the Social Security payroll tax to at least 15 per cent, half to be paid by the employee.

Before I had any thought of coming to Washington, in the Spring of 1960 I authored a magazine article giving the reasons for my opposition to Medicare. After I took office, the bitterly anti-Medicare American Medical Association gleefully reprinted the article in their Journal and various anti-Medicare Congressmen inserted it in the Congressional Record.

I wasn't the only new Cabinet member whose past writings were dredged up in an effort to embarrass him. Dean Rusk in earlier years had written, in gentle reproof of John Foster Dulles' globe-trotting, that the Secretary of State should stay at home and mind the store. But Dean ended up doing plenty of globe-trotting himself. Arthur Goldberg as a labor lawyer had attacked the Taft-

Hartley Act and urged its repeal. But when he became Secretary of Labor, he used it.

There were more startling examples from previous administrations of Cabinet members who did not agree with everything in their President's program. Cordell Hull was Franklin Roosevelt's Secretary of State for eleven years, although he disagreed with a large part of the New Deal domestic program. At Cabinet meetings he just kept his mouth shut about the many proposals he disagreed with.

I made more political speeches on behalf of the Administration while I was in office than any other Cabinet officer, but Medicare was the one topic on which I declined to speak. No one ever pressed me to support it or to speak on it, but others were so pressed. In 1962, in the Administration's great effort to stir up grass-roots support for the program, speakers were sent out from Washington to rallies throughout the country. The turnouts were generally disappointing, however, and the support whipped up did not appear too spontaneous. I happened to catch on television a sidewalk interviewer as he asked one woman why she was there. She didn't hesitate a second. "The union called me up and told me to get right down here," she said. "I didn't know what for, but here I am."

There is always a great effort made to stir up support for what the Administration sees as its "must bills," which supposedly have a great deal of glamor and political appeal, but which almost inevitably involve large appropriations. Money is siphoned off for them, leaving the traditional, conventional, established, nonglamorous Federal agencies subjected to an unhealthy squeeze for funds. A dramatic example of this is the inability of the 175-year-old Customs Bureau to get the money it needs for an adequate crackdown on narcotics smuggling. Some day, budget pressure on the Post Office may well force the end of Saturday mail delivery, although it would save only an insignificant amount compared to the six million dollars the Defense Department spends *every hour!*

The Kennedy programs caused much comment, but the Administration itself inspired an untold number of jokes and stories.

Eighteen months after the Kennedys took office, cracks about touch football were still good for an uproarious laugh. There was still a big response to worn-out jokes about Bobby in 1968, Teddy in 1976, and then it's Caroline in 1984. Talk of splitting the President's home state into High Mass. and Low Mass. convulsed crowds with laughter. The new definition of GOP (Genuflect or Perish) was resurrected from Al Smith days.

But one story is fresh. It involves a lady in Kansas who came into the local post office shortly after the 1960 election and asked for 50 cents worth of stamps.

"What denomination?" asked the clerk.

"Well, I didn't know it had come to that," the woman snapped. "Baptist."

Chapter 11
THE VIEW FROM
THE LIMOUSINE WINDOW

The Constitution doesn't even mention the Cabinet. The extent to which he uses this group is entirely up to the President.

Members of the public, to the extent they think about it at all, think of the Cabinet as meeting often and deliberating with the President on the whole range of government problems, domestic and international. They may even have a vague idea that votes are taken on the various issues although some will recall the story about Lincoln's decision which was taken contrary to the unanimous vote of his Cabinet: "Seven noes, one aye—the ayes have it."

Andrew Jackson largely ignored his official Cabinet, preferring a "kitchen cabinet" of his own choosing. Abraham Lincoln and Woodrow Wilson did not like the idea of regular Cabinet meetings. Shortly after one of Lincoln's Cabinet members resigned, an acquaintance asked Lincoln why he did not get rid of all seven members of his Cabinet. The President replied:

"Well, you know, there was a farmer in Illinois who was much troubled with skunks. One moonlight night he loaded his old shot-gun and hid behind the wood-pile. Before long there appeared not one skunk but *seven*. Said the farmer: 'I took aim, blazed away, killed one, but he raised such a fearful smell that I concluded it was best to let the other six go.'"

A Wilson Cabinet member reported that for weeks during one period the Cabinet spent its time "largely in telling stories."

Two of Franklin Roosevelt's Cabinet members agreed that Cabinet meetings, as conducted in that period, were a waste of time.

95

President Eisenhower once said, "In Cabinet meetings I always wait for George Humphrey to speak. I sit back and listen to the others talk while he doesn't say anything. But I know that when he speaks he will say just what I am thinking."

Many Presidents have found that it is pointless to take a vote in a Cabinet meeting and that the Cabinet is ineffective as a decision-making body.

During the thirty-one months that I was Postmaster General, President Kennedy called only twenty-six Cabinet meetings, an average of one every five weeks. Many of the meetings were largely perfunctory. The most highly publicized (at the time of the Cuban missile crisis) lasted but ten minutes; others were as short as half an hour. For one three-month period (November 9, 1961–February 8, 1962) the Cabinet did not meet at all.

The Cabinet first met on January 26, in the week immediately after the Inauguration. Each officer talked of the principal problems and issues immediately ahead, and the meeting lasted for two hours. It could have provided a pattern for meaningful meetings on a regular basis; yet only one other time—and that on July 3, 1963, two and a half years later—was each individual Cabinet officer called on to talk about whatever was on his mind.

Why this dearth of dialogue? Certainly a major factor was that the men President Kennedy chose for his Cabinet did not fall easily and naturally into line with his "one man band" approach to running the Government. Three of them—Luther Hodges, Orville Freeman and Abraham Ribicoff—had been successful and forceful Governors of states. In addition, Ribicoff had served in Congress, as had Stewart Udall. Arthur Goldberg had for many years been a big name on the labor scene and in Washington. These five plus myself made up the six members of the "domestic Cabinet." (Technically also a member of the domestic group, Robert Kennedy participated importantly in foreign policy with Dean Rusk, Robert McNamara and Douglas Dillon, in addition to having a unique position in other respects.)

None of us was a cigar-store Indian. Yet President Kennedy had never had the experience of being an executive among lesser but by no means subservient executives; he had been served by a fanatically devoted band of men of his own creation. His Cabinet was a different run of shad. Each member was independent and quick to express his views, perhaps too much so for the President's taste. At any rate, he soon began to exhibit restlessness and impatience during Cabinet meetings, which thereafter diminished in frequency. After the first meeting only a week had passed before he called another, on February 2. Then he let a month go by, to March 2, before calling the third. The next one, on April 20, took place after an interval of seven weeks.

Still, I believe the President planned to have more frequent Cabinet meetings. On April 6, 1961, I sent a note to Fred Dutton, Secretary of the Cabinet, requesting "some tentative idea of the dates on which there might be Cabinet meetings," as it would be helpful to me in planning out-of-town trips. He replied that the next meeting would take place April 13 (it did not) and every other Thursday thereafter, "subject to the President's schedule for meetings with the foreign leaders coming to this country."

Columnist Charles Bartlett, considered a Kennedy intimate, said that as late as November, 1961, the President was still talking about having Cabinet meetings every other week. On at least two occasions that year the President mentioned at Cabinet sessions that he planned to hold them more frequently and more regularly. At an early meeting he told those present to telephone him or Lyndon Johnson on anything of importance, to "err on the side of referring too much" on policy matters. But before long the remark at the opening of a Cabinet session was likely to be that he was pressed for time and would have to limit the meeting to an hour; or to keep it short, that he was busy.

In May, 1961, President Kennedy invited his Cabinet to the weekly White House breakfast with Democratic Congressional leaders, but the invitation was never repeated. Some members spoke out on their own initiative at that time, and I had the feeling that such independence was not welcome. That same spring the President stated in a television interview that he thought Cabinet meetings were a waste of time. The impression was created (and reported as fact by knowledgeable columnists) that the President preferred smaller meetings with those Cabinet

members concerned with a specific problem. But his absorption
with politics, publicity, and foreign policy allowed him little time
to be concerned about the domestic departments, unless they had
an immediate political aspect. For the domestic Cabinet, personal
meetings with the President became fewer and farther between,
and more than one member grew increasingly unhappy because
it was so difficult to see the President.

The atmosphere at Cabinet meetings should have been right
for free-and-easy, frank discussion. At the outset it had been
only natural to assume that such discussion would be encouraged.
In contrast to the Eisenhower Cabinet—at which the sheer number of staff members present hampered discussion—under President Kennedy there were usually only five persons in the room
besides the President himself, his ten Cabinet members, the Vice
President, and Adlai Stevenson on the few occasions when he
could attend. These five were the Director of the Budget, originally David Bell, later Kermit Gordon; the Chairman of the
Council of Economic Advisers, Walter Heller; the Chairman of
the Civil Service Commission, John Macy; Special Counsel Ted
Sorensen; and the Secretary of the Cabinet, originally Fred
Dutton and later Ted Reardon. They did not sit at the Cabinet
table and, aside from Heller, seldom said anything unless called
upon.

The setting may have been right, but after the first two or three
meetings one had the distinct impression that the President felt
that decisions on major matters were not made—or even influenced—at Cabinet sessions, and that discussion there was a waste
of time. (The Washington *Post* once quoted the President as
illustrating his attitude toward Cabinet meetings by saying he
would consider it a waste of time to discuss Vietnam with the
Postmaster General. I suppose—or at least I *hope*—he used this
only as an example!) When members spoke up to suggest or to
discuss major Administration policy, the President would listen
with thinly disguised impatience and then postpone or otherwise
bypass the question, usually on the grounds that we were too
rushed to go into it. For example, at a meeting early in 1963,
Budget Director Gordon presented some charts showing how
Government spending must be reduced in order to achieve the

goal of a balanced budget. Two Cabinet members, favoring more
Federal spending to aid the economy, requested a full discussion
of budget policy. I was marshalling ammunition against their
position when the President said that we would discuss it when
more time was available. That is the last the Cabinet ever heard
of it. On another occasion that winter, a very knowledgeable
Cabinet member warned that the Administration was going too
far too fast on civil rights for it not to hurt politically. This, too,
elicited the typical Kennedy response: a very polite, noncom-
mittal remark which did not encourage further discussion of the
subject.

Of course the President was, without exception, personally gra-
cious and courteous, even charming, and he could inject his justly
famed wit into the most dismal of situations. At the opening of a
Cabinet meeting held at the time of the debacle at the Bay of Pigs
the President said to his domestic Cabinet members, "You are all
lucky. You knew nothing about it in advance so you don't have
to take any of the blame." When he was attacked for appointing
his brother to head the Department of Justice, he made the now-
famous quip, "I don't know why I should be criticized for giving
my brother a little legal experience before he goes out to practice
law." His was the disarming quality of turning criticism into a
joke on himself.

Whenever I saw the President informally in his office he was
the same warm, friendly, easy-to-talk-to personality that had at-
tracted me at our first meeting in 1959. These occasions were few;
the President gave me an almost free hand in running the Post
Office and considered frequent consultations unnecessary. The
first took place soon after the Inauguration, when I met with him
and Ted Sorensen to appeal a White House decision to seek a
higher postal rate increase than I considered desirable or likely to
win Congressional approval. The President and Ted were inclined to give a very stiff increase to magazine rates, but I felt the
total increase package they wanted on rates other than first class
was too severe. I did not win my argument.

About ten persons were present at a later meeting with the
President concerning the Post Office Department's efforts to increase the allowable size and weight of parcel post. The Depart-

ment's purpose was to gain a greater share of the profitable large parcel business so as to avoid a radical increase in the rates for smaller packages. The President asked perceptive questions and very soon picked up the essential points of a highly complex problem. (The problem had a specific political overtone, involving railroad unions, and was not just "Post Office.") For reasons that he considered impelling, he could not go along with my proposal. As the meeting broke up he demonstrated his memorable graciousness by saying, in the presence of the others, "Ed, I'm sorry not to be able to go along with you on this parcel post problem, because I disagreed with you last year on the amount of postal rate increase we should ask for and, as it's turned out, you were right." (The proposal the President had required me to present to the House Post Office Committee in 1961 didn't get any place at all. The more modest request I had urged him to accept was passed by Congress in 1962 and we entered the era of the 5-cent stamp.)

My duties as Postmaster General kept me away from Washington a lot of the time. My first year as Postmaster General I traveled 70,000 miles, held thirty-five full-fledged press conferences, and each month delivered about ten speeches. I also estimate that I rode in the back seat of at least thirty big, black Cadillac limousines belonging to the same number of funeral parlors.

I did not, as you might suppose, attend thirty funerals. I was simply the victim of motorcade madness wherever I traveled. Motorcade madness—the only apt cognomen for that affliction of the mind—affects police departments and welcoming committees throughout the United States. It becomes apparent to a Cabinet member in his travels that cities all over the country measure their prestige by the speed and noise of the motorcycle escort they can provide visiting dignitaries.

I have been rushed at eighty miles per hour the twenty miles from Edgewater to Newark, New Jersey, despite my pleas and protests that I was in no rush at all—indeed, after arriving, thankfully, in Newark I had two hours to kill before my engagement. I

have sped behind gleeful police escorts through crowded sections
of Detroit and Chicago and cities whose names I have long since
forgotten, cities of which my most lasting impressions are of the
screaming sirens and flashing lights of the always unnecessary
and invariably unpleasant motorcades. The look of each place is a
blur through a windshield, an unfocused series of gray buildings
on the other side of motorcycle policemen who scatter people like
so many chickens back to the curbings. I never did go to a
funeral on one of those trips, but I always felt that I might be
plummeting along at eighty per, to my own. Years ago, when
Adlai Stevenson was Governor of Illinois, he and I were rushed
into Springfield, Missouri, behind screaming sirens. The car ran
over a dog on the way. It might have been a child, a possibility I
have often pondered during similar headlong dashes.

For sheer terror I never expected to see the equal of a speeding
American motorcade. Then in 1963 I went to Paris as the head of
the American delegation to the International Postal Conference. I
can state unequivocally that the Paris version of the suicidal rush
excels all others within my ken. Our conference group went
everywhere in twenty limousines escorted by an equal number of
daring motorcycle policemen, each equipped with a loud, multi-
note horn—a pleasant change, by the way, from our shrill sirens.
As we sped through the city's intersections and red lights at
breakneck speed and on the wrong side of the street, the policemen would race ahead, hands off the handlebars and arms extended to either side to hold back onrushing traffic. My English
counterpart quailed at this show of authority and said that if they
tried that in London there would be a riot. I have no doubt that
he spoke the truth. When we got to London we had a single
police outrider for one brief excursion, and he seemed intent on
giving the impression he had no connection of any sort with our
party.

The wining and dining provided by our Parisian hosts made
our own Post Office Department's entertaining look impover-
ished by comparison. European post offices have much more
money to spend on such niceties than does ours, in part because
European postal departments also run the highly profitable tele-

phone and telegraph systems—keeping the revenue they collect, instead of having to do battle with their legislative bodies for each year's operating appropriations.

My last evening in Paris I had one free hour before the wild ride to the airport. I wanted to see the Louvre, which I had last seen in 1932, and I wanted to make my way there alone, without police escort. When I finally breached the Paris traffic in a taxi, it was half an hour after closing time. People were entering, however, for a special press preview of a Delacroix exhibit. I revived my high school French at the museum's office and came into possession of a press pass, which allowed me one of the few quiet and unescorted moments of my visit to the City of Light.

On the flight to Europe, Trans-World Airlines had furnished each of its passengers with a small plastic case containing a toothbrush, toothpaste, and a face cloth which I took along when I got off the plane. In Frankfort, which we visited on the same trip, our German postal friends put us up in what was once a palace and is now a very elegant hotel. On the edge of the enormous bathtub in my splendid suite I left the TWA washcloth. Later, when all of us were getting into cars to head for our next destination, a porter came rushing out, much excited, looking for me. The small package he delivered contained the TWA washcloth.

In Hamburg I left it on the side of the tub again, but, unknown to me, just before our departure, a conscientious maid carefully placed the soggy thing on top of the papers in my dispatch case where I did not discover it until our arrival in West Berlin. I may still have that TWA cloth someplace.

Another fond memory of TWA concerns its in-flight motion pictures. Bursting with enthusiasm, the four of us in the American delegation to the International Postal Conference boarded our flight to Paris determined to spread good will and make friends for the United States among the officials from other countries. Such sanguine thoughts hardly prepared us for that night's bill—*The Ugly American*.

One day the State Department phoned to suggest I make a good-will trip to Senegal, Liberia, and the Ivory Coast in order to help the people of those countries improve their postal systems. Margery Michelmore, a young Peace Corps recruit, had just dropped a post card in Nigeria, and demonstrated (when the post card was construed to be critical of Nigerian conditions, and set off an international incident) that the postal system there could stand a little beefing up, too. So, hoping to end our conversation on a humorous note, I said to the State Department official, "Are you sure you don't want me to go to Nigeria, too, and check on their handling of post cards?"

The next day the man called back and said yes, they would like me to include Nigeria. This added to my doubts as to whether Africa was really eagerly awaiting my guidance on its postal problems, and I decided I could do more for good mail service by staying home and helping to prepare for the Christmas rush then impending.

International trips to promote good will often contain unexpected—and, what's worse, unsuspected—risks. Before we went to Japan to represent the President at the Osaka International Trade Fair, Post Office Department photographers came out to the house to take pictures of Mrs. Day. Since the Fair's theme was food and food preparation, she would be billed prominently in the Fair, and the pictures were to be sent to Osaka for advance publicity. Mrs. Day was posed standing before some book shelves, and the pictures came out beautifully. At the last minute, however, as they were being wrapped for mailing to Japan, Jim Kelleher noticed that in every one of them the title of one book on the shelves in the background stood out clearly. The book was *Day of Infamy,* the story of the Japanese attack on Pearl Harbor. Needless to say, the pictures were taken again, without *Day of Infamy.*

A wife, the most valuable aide of all in creating good will on an official trip abroad, is also a financial problem. A Cabinet member can take a number of official aides at government expense, but he's got to pay out of his own pocket for his wife. When Arthur Goldberg was Secretary of Labor he urged the government to change all that. He pointed out that both husband and wife could travel tourist class and it wouldn't cost much more than it does for one alone in first class. To prove his point, he took Mrs. Goldberg and they both flew tourist class on a visit to the Scandinavian countries. Waiting to welcome them when they landed was a distinguished crowd of officials, embassy personnel, labor leaders, reporters, and what not, all lined up along a red carpet which had been unrolled for the Goldbergs. The carpet, of course, swept up unswervingly to the first class exit. The Goldbergs embarked from the tourist section in the back of the plane. The confusion that ensued was considerable.

On a non-governmental flight between Los Angeles and Washington my wife caused confusion on a smaller scale when she disappeared for an extended length of time. The stewardess, a sweet girl from the South, was embarrassed to find that the lock on the washroom door was stuck and Mrs. Day couldn't get out. "Why couldn't that have happened to a Senatuh's wife?" she drawled.

In the course of traveling some seventy thousand miles each year as Postmaster General, I visited scores of post offices in 35 states. In Hawaii I drank Scotch from a teapot thoughtfully provided by Governor Quinn, after I had spent the cocktail hour shaking hands with 800 Hawaiian postal workers. In Seattle, I persuaded the operators of the "Post Office Loan Company" to change the name of their establishment, directly opposite the main Federal building, and to give their huge sign to the Post Office Department. Once the last two words had been removed, the sign was sent up to Girdwood, Alaska. I had noticed that the post office there had only a small, cardboard identification; now it boasts a sign as big as the whole building. During a flight from Wichita to San Francisco the plane jolted through a series of storms so severe that the light fixtures shook loose and hung down from the ceiling. The captain's advice: "Be sure your seat belts are tight. Remain calm. Don't act nervous, it makes the stewardesses nervous. And if you have any questions, ask the stewardesses. They're questionable."

After a trip to Montana I received a letter from a woman in Great Falls, which read:

After seeing your picture in our local paper last Tuesday, I am wondering where I have seen you before. Are you the J. Edward Day, mentioned in the article that was in Montana last week?

Will you kindly tell me if it was you who called on my husband and I about a roofing job, recently.

If so, I only wish I had known that I was talking to such a V.I.P. I am afraid that I would have been struck speechless, which would have been a good thing, don't you think?

My appearance on John Daly's television show, "What's My Line," prompted a letter addressed to J. Edward Daly inquiring whether I was John Daly's brother. At least it didn't say father.

In Los Angeles in the fall of 1962 I celebrated a free afternoon between political and postal speeches by going to the opening day of the beautiful Hollywood Park Racetrack. There I was photographed with a young lady I had never seen before. The results appeared in the paper the next day. Unknown to me, Tony Celebrezze, the Secretary of Health, Education and Welfare, was busily making speeches in Los Angeles that same day. Several weeks later at a luncheon gathering of the Cabinet in Washington, he told how hard he had been working in Los Angeles and how many speeches he had made on behalf of the Democratic Party. He said that he, of course, assumed that I had been doing the same. Then he produced the picture of me "having a gay old time" at the track. "And there are no votes out there," he concluded, "but neigh votes."

In Cincinnati I introduced ABCD mail service at a sidewalk ceremony in front of the Post Office. In the midst of the television cameras, news photographers, and a sizable crowd of postal people and bystanders, a colorful looking hobo with a curly beard appeared at my elbow. From his battered satchel he took a pair of hedge clippers and suggested that I use them to trim his whiskers. I demurred, but to show there were no hard feelings I reached out to shake hands with him. He grabbed my hand and, bowing elaborately, kissed it, to the vast amusement of the crowd.

The following day at the Memphis Post Office I ran across a clerk who, disgusted at women's bobbed hair, had sworn never to cut his again. By the time of my visit it was tied in a pony-tail and reached to the floor. If I could have gotten him together with the hobo and the hedge clippers, it would have been a service to the tonsorial arts. Perhaps, too, the desire for publicity in both of them would have been satisfied.

There's no question about it—the life of a traveling salesman, whether for Fuller Brushes, the Democratic Party, or the Post Office, is fraught with perils undreamt of by the home folks.

Senator Warren Magnuson and I visited Seattle to attend issuing ceremonies for a stamp commemorating that city's Century 21 World's Fair. I ended up by lifting a letter from the United States Mails and taking a bow in a burlesque theater. Neither act was at all hard to arrange; each just happened, unfortunately.

The morning we were to bring out the stamp at the Fair, a local newspaper carried a story to the effect that a highlight of the scheduled ceremonies would be a congratulatory letter from President Kennedy that I would present to Senator Magnuson.

"Where's the letter?" I asked the Senator, in considerable surprise. "This is the first I've heard about it."

The Senator, his assistant, and the postal staff were all equally in the dark. No one had heard anything about it and no one seemed to know where the newspaper story had originated. But the story was specific and in a couple of hours, at the ceremony at the Space Needle Post Office, reporters would want to see that letter and use it as a gimmick for pictures and stories. We thought about typing up a letter and clearing it with the White House by telephone, but letterheads and signature were three thousand miles away.

Then we decided to tell the reporters that the advance publicity on the letter was generally correct but inaccurate in detail; the letter was in fact *from* Senator Magnuson *to* President Kennedy, and it was going to be the first item mailed from the post office in the Space Needle. In the rush no one had time to compose a letter to the President, so we ended up with a blank sheet of paper inside one of Senator Magnuson's official envelopes addressed to the White House.

When the picture taking started, the letter was the center of attention. The Senator and I pushed it through the mail slot; then someone ran into the building, retrieved the letter and we went through the whole business again. And again. And again, because each newspaper wanted its own pose, and then we included a couple of run-throughs for television. The reporters, of course, wanted to know what the letter said. The Senator extemporized beautifully. Never has so much well-phrased content been attributed to one blank sheet of paper.

When it was all over someone said, "What are they going to think at the White House when they receive that envelope from Senator Magnuson with no letter in it?" But the letter was safely in my briefcase, and there it stayed. No one had noticed that in all that mailing and retrieving there was one more retrieval than return.

Our hosts at the Fair thought we should relax that night with a visit to another section of the grounds. Now almost every World's Fair has a Little Egypt, a Sally Rand or something comparably eye-opening, but in staid Seattle that presented a problem. Fair management solved it by taking the Seattle officials concerned with standards of exposure to Las Vegas to see what was done in the big time. The gambit worked, because the show we saw at the theater-restaurant was right up—or should I say down?—to Las Vegas standards.

I had hoped to remain unobtrusively in the back of that establishment, but before I could stop them, some eager beavers shooed the occupants from a table in front center and ensconced us there forthwith, just across the footlights from the undulating female performers. The place was dark, so things could have been worse—and, sure enough, they soon were. When the show was nearly over, a buxom mistress of ceremonies appeared, grabbed the microphone and blared:

"And now I want to introduce for a bow a distinguished visitor we are proud to have with us tonight, the distinguished Postmaster General of the United States!!!" Trumpets, fanfares, and flourishes.

I wanted to slip quietly under the table, but the spotlight found me instantly.

A trip to Milwaukee and environs illustrated several more of the snares a traveling official can fall into. I went there on the eve of Labor Day, 1961, for the express purpose of dedicating the Workman's Compensation commemorative stamp, but by the time I arrived I was signed up for four more speeches in four more cities, and a luncheon meeting with local political leaders. Then an early morning tour of possible sites for a new post office was proposed, very casually, very incidentally, just to help kill the time in case I should be hanging around at eight in the morning with nothing to think about but those five speeches ahead. The tour turned out to be an enormous safari composed of two busloads of city officials, Chamber of Commerce bigwigs, real estate people, a Congressman, miscellaneous hangers-on, and the ever-present newsmen, all munching doughnuts on the bus. I was completely in the dark about any new Milwaukee Post Office; I didn't even know if one were planned. But it seemed that a railroad company was particularly anxious to have us take an unwanted passenger station off its hands.

Before I knew it, I had been hustled into a railroad car, set down in front of a collection of maps and drawings and, surrounded by television cameras, reporters and interested parties from every civic echelon, was cross-examined about the new post office. Apparently hints from the Post Office Department had ignited expectations in Milwaukee, and the whole thing had gone much, much further than anyone had bothered to tell me about.

Anyway, I said bright-eyed and innocent into the microphones: "I'm not sure we're going to build a new post office in Milwaukee at all."

Suddenly I knew how Marshal Pétain felt, surrounded by the enemy on a railroad car. Such incredulous gasps, groans, snarls, mutterings, and hurried cover-up statements from city officials, the Congressman, and others! And Milwaukee *is* getting a new post office, by the way.

After fleeing from the railroad car, feeling lucky to escape with only mental scars, I got down to the main business of my visit: dedicating the new Workman's Compensation stamp, and presenting a special set of the stamps to an elderly gentleman who supposedly had been in the Wisconsin State Legislature in 1911 when the first Workman's Compensation Law in the country was passed. The gentleman accepted the stamps with pleasure. It was only later that we found out that so someone had slipped up in the research department. The man who got the stamps had not been in the Wisconsin legislature in 1911. Or any other year, for that matter.

The stamps disposed of, we flew by private plane to Racine and Kenosha and a couple of other towns at which I regaled preoccupied Labor Day picnic crowds with stirring speeches. At one place I competed unsuccessfully with loudly amplified music from a nearby carousel. At another, a county fair race track, the crowd had already left when we arrived. My keepers even wanted to fly me up to Green Bay to make a brief speech at the Packers' football game, but there I put my foot down. I remembered that my friend Dick Daley, before he became mayor of Chicago, warned me that men do not attend sporting events to hear speeches by public officials. They will usually boo on general principles, he said. That would have been all I'd needed that day.

Hotel stops on such trips are often a nightmare for a Cabinet member. I refer to the difficulty of traveling on a 16-dollar-a-day expense allowance. Local welcoming committees take as much pride in reserving the very finest suite in the very finest hotel as they do in the number of Cadillacs in the motor procession. Many times after being deposited in a fancy suite and thanking the committee I hurriedly called the front desk to insist on being moved to something more modest. It is impossible to pay 60 or 80 dollars a night for an elegant suite on a 16-dollar allowance, and it is no favor to have the local committee pick up the tab. Sherman Adams tried it now and then, and we all know what happened to him.

In a Los Angeles hotel I made the mistake of thinking that my door locked automatically, and I went to bed without turning the key. The next morning my wallet was still there, but empty. The same thing happened that night to other guests, including the Swedish Ambassador. The hotel manager was not in, but his assistant listened to my story, then dispensed a modicum of sympathy and a reprimand: "You should have realized that in a prestige hotel such as this there are never automatic locks. They are used only in"—there was an audible sneer—"*commercial* hotels."

The manager returned as I was leaving his office and invited me to repeat my tale of woe. His sympathy was of a different complexion: "We are sorry about not having automatic locks. We should have them, but we found it would cost 30,000 dollars to do a complete job throughout the hotel. What would you accept as a reasonable cash settlement?" (The incident confirmed to my traveling companions that I was economy minded. I knew exactly how much had been in my wallet because I knew to the penny what was in it on arrival in Los Angeles two mornings before, and I had spent only 4 dollars in the interim.)

My experience with hotel-hopping has convinced me that automatic elevators are an abomination. In Omaha I was stranded between floors in an elevator that would budge neither up nor down. When we finally got the door open, we had to crawl out one by one through a space about three feet high. As I climbed out, praying that the elevator wouldn't start upward, a picture of a bacon slicer in a butcher shop emblazoned itself on my mind. I couldn't dislodge that either.

Perhaps the strangest encounter I ever had in a hotel was at the Peabody in Memphis, where I ran into a dozen large ducks standing around a fountain in the lobby. My local hosts explained that the ducks are on duty in shifts. At a designated signal they walk unattended to a waiting elevator and ride up to a "penthouse" on the roof where they spend the time until their next stint on the job. When I expressed some surprise at this undoubtedly unique arrangement, I was assured that the ducks are also allowed summer vacations—which is probably how the expression "everything's ducky" originated.

The Coronado near San Diego is a popular convention hotel, although it is more than eighty years old. It is an ornate frame building of great charm. But despite that, and despite its incomparable ocean-front setting, some first-time guests are disconcerted by the apparent fire hazard. Then they notice the signs throughout the building proclaiming that it contains 5,000 sprinklers. I once opened a convention speech there with a suggestion that before going to sleep each guest should say this prayer:

> Now I lay me down to sleep,
> While the sprinklers their vigil keep;
> I will rest quite unconcerned,
> I may get wet but I won't get burned.

I should have been careful, of course, speaking of prayers as a public official. After the Supreme Court's ruling against prayers in public schools, I often wondered if the Post Office might become embroiled in controversy over the cancellation, "Pray for Peace," which was authorized by statute. I cannot think of that landmark decision without recalling the story about the teacher who sneezed in school. When one of her little students said "God bless you," the teacher replied, "Shut up or you'll get us both in trouble." Or the "Peanuts" cartoon showing the little girl checking to see that the windows were closed and that no one was listening behind the door or the sofa before she whispered to her little friend, "We prayed in school today."

In May, 1962, I set out for Beatrice, Nebraska, to dedicate a stamp to commemorate the hundredth anniversary of the Homestead Act. When my plane arrived at Omaha a large delegation of local dignitaries and reporters and photographers was waiting at the bottom of the ramp. I was pleasantly surprised at such a turnout, but I should have known better. Nebraska is usually the most Republican state in the Union and the crowd was there to greet a Republican Congressman who was also on the plane. As reporters crowded around him and flashbulbs popped, I skirted the delegation unnoticed and made my way to the terminal, feeling about as welcome in Nebraska as a skunk at a lawn party.

Some local bigwigs finally took me in tow and ushered me aboard—you guessed it—a big, black, chauffeur-driven Cadillac borrowed, probably, from a funeral parlor. In the next thirty-six hours this automobile became more than a casual acquaintance.

We drove to Lincoln the next morning, picked up the Governor (oddly enough, a Democrat), and proceeded to Beatrice. The ceremonies were held there in a huge, unpainted frame shed referred to grandly as a "Chataqua [sic] tabernacle." I was told that William Jennings Bryan had delivered orations there. The building must have been old even then.

In the middle of my remarks, a spider crawled over my hand, up my arm, and across my neck. The alert master of ceremonies, a local businessman named Willkie, sprang to his feet and swept the creature away so deftly that I didn't miss a phrase. But that was only a preliminary test of my aplomb.

Shortly afterward and with absolutely no warning, a bird's nest fell from a rafter in the hall onto the head of a man in the audience. The nest was empty, fortunately, so no one could say that my speech had laid an egg. I finished it, thankful that the building still stood, and spent the next half hour autographing first-day covers for stamp collectors, shaking hands with visiting postmasters and politicians, and posing for pictures. Finally we boarded the Cadillac, and there was another round of handshaking from the window, then much waving. One might have thought we were leaving Beatrice for the moon. Finally, we were all set. The police escort—sirens ready to wail—was waiting, an expectant crowd lined the drive. But the borrowed Cadillac wouldn't budge. It had a dead battery.

We transferred to the sheriff's car for the ride to the airport, under a darkening sky. By the time we arrived the heavens looked ominous indeed, but the pilot of the little two-seater was a game bird. "There are some cyclones along the route but I *think* we can make it," he said, with a faint attempt at cheer in his voice.

We decided to get a new battery for the borrowed Cadillac and proceeded on our way through gale and cloudburst in that somber vehicle, taking it several hundred miles farther from its home-based funeral parlor.

Chapter 12
TALKING
TURKEY

ONE DAY the head of a large organization stopped by my office with a persuasive and highly flattering plea for me to make a speech at his group's annual dinner. The board of directors had unanimously decided that I was the man best qualified to address their organization, my petitioner said. Naturally they had considered many names, but mine was the one they always came back to. They knew, of course, that I would have a particularly significant message for them. Etc., etc., etc.

"What date did you say the dinner is to be?" I asked.

"October 26th."

"I'm terribly sorry, but I already have a commitment for that night," I said, after checking my calendar.

"Gosh," said my visitor, who'd apparently never matriculated at Dale Carnegie's, "everyone we've asked has a previous commitment for that night."

A former president of the National Press Club stands out as an example of how not to introduce a speaker once you get him. Before introducing me at a Press Club luncheon, this Washington scribe had checked the press clippings concerning changes I was making in the Post Office. He checked the clippings so carefully and related their facts so fully to the audience that there was nothing left for me to say. When I was finally allowed to speak, I ventured to observe: "A good master of ceremonies should be like a fan dancer's fan: he should call attention to the subject without trying to cover it."

One of the most unfortunate introductions I've ever heard of was the attempt of former Speaker of the House Joe Martin to present Syngman Rhee, then President of South Korea, to a joint session of Congress. "It is a distinct honor and privilege to present to you the distinguished President of India," said Martin. His tones rang through the legislative chamber, immediately followed by a rush of murmurs. One of them reached Martin's ear. "I mean the President of Indiana," he said, apparently already concerned with the political machinations of Charles Halleck, who soon replaced Martin as Republican leader in the House.

Enough of introductions—the speech itself is the story, and sometimes it's a very long one. Whenever I hear a Protestant minister giving a long, drawn-out invocation I figure the Protestants are still trying to get equal time for the lengthy invocation given by Cardinal Cushing at President Kennedy's Inauguration.

Every speaker should remember the advice of the old man to his son: "When you speak in public, do not forget to stand up so that people can see you, speak in a loud voice so that they can hear you, and above all, my boy, do not forget to be brief, so that they may be grateful to you."

Perhaps my best speech—certainly my briefest—was one I had nothing to do with, although it was given in my name. Shortly before Christmas, 1960, the Chicago law firm with which Adlai Stevenson and I had been associated held its annual luncheon. I couldn't make it to Chicago, but Adlai did, and said to the assemblage: "Ed Day was extremely sorry he couldn't be here. But as you know, he is getting ready to take on the incredibly difficult job of running our great postal system. Even so, he wanted me personally to bring you a message from him. It is a matter about which he feels very deeply."

With that Adlai pulled a crumpled piece of paper from his pocket, smoothed it, adjusted his glasses, and read aloud: "Write legibly."

Some of my own speeches provoked less jolly reactions. When it seemed that everybody in the Kennedy Administration but Pierre Salinger and me was taking fifty-mile hikes, I put my tongue in my cheek and mentioned that it was no wonder so many people in the Kennedy Administration had taken up walking in a big way—there are a lot of big shoe factories in Massachusetts.

A newspaper in Hartford, Connecticut, picked this out of my speech, believe it or not, and editorialized angrily that I had spilled the beans on yet another sinister Kennedy family scheme to advance their political fortunes in their own state.

Another time, shortly after Governor Rockefeller married Mrs. Murphy, I noted that the Governor had learned from the Kennedys the political value of an Irish name in the family. Very shortly afterward I received a three-page, single-spaced, typewritten letter from a man I did not know who tried to show me, with extensive documentation, that Kennedy is not an Irish name at all but a Scottish one. And O'Brien, I suppose, is Yiddish.

There were loud protests in Philadelphia when I made some less than devout remarks about the local patron saint, Benjamin Franklin, postmaster of that city for twenty years and also first Postmaster General of the United States. "Ben," I said, "was kind to his relatives—he put five of them on the Post Office payroll."

After I was quoted in the Philadelphia papers, an organization of advertising men from that city, called the Poor Richard Club, took exception in the press to my remarks about their hero, which were accurate enough. Observing that Ben at least ran the Post Office without a deficit, they asked me to return to Philadelphia to account for my statements before a meeting of their organization. They even offered to pay my way.

I saw that I had goofed terribly in departing from a reverent, prayerful attitude toward Philadelphia's hero. I of course knew better than to return to the scene of my crime, so I wrote them:

"I hereby solemnly swear, on a copy of *Poor Richard's Almanac,* that I will never, never, ever mention that:

1) George Washington didn't really cut down that cherry tree;
2) Abraham Lincoln didn't really write the Gettysburg Address on the back of an envelope;
3) Ben Franklin wasn't really stuffy and pompous but had a sense of humor and some human frailties;
4) Postmaster Franklin could operate the Post Office in the black because in those days they didn't have a low subsidized postage rate for advertising circulars."

My inability to accept their invitation I ascribed to the rewriting of a St. Patrick's Day speech. "You see, in the first draft I mentioned, quite unpardonably, that St. Patrick wasn't really an Irishman," I explained.

Anyone who's writing a speech is indeed well advised to stay away from satire of the local deities. I must confess, however, that I occasionally lapse from this wise dictum myself, as when I addressed the 1962 Postmasters' Convention in Pittsburgh. I said, "The late Frank Lloyd Wright, the great American architect, came to Pittsburgh a score or so years ago as a consultant on city planning. After looking over the city, Mr. Wright came up with this terse bit of advice: 'Abandon it.'"

When I got around to my speech to the Friendly Sons of St. Patrick, though, I was careful to observe the amenities. I even put in a good word for Ben Franklin, "a most gregarious and out-going gentleman—a great joiner of good causes and good organizations," I said. "So I expect he may well have been one of the early day adherents of the Friendly Sons of St. Patrick because he originally came from Boston. And the first known celebration of St. Patrick's Day in America took place in Boston in 1737." The celebration was by a group called the Charitable Irish Society, which was organized by leading Irish Protestants. The organization still exists, but now its membership is almost 100 per cent Catholic.

The Irish and Ben Franklin gave me lots to talk about. I told that same group that the Pennsylvania Line, the famous Revolutionary Army corps, was so solidly Irish that Light Horse Harry Lee renamed it "the line to Ireland." It was small wonder then that when Lord Cornwallis's surrender was announced to the British Parliament, Lord Mountjoy said, "England has lost America through the exertions of Irish immigrants." The Irish problem was to concern Parliament for a long, long time.

As for Franklin, I found many occasions to mention him. In the years before the Revolutionary War, the Colonists began to rebel against the attempts of the British to make a profit on the postal service. As a result, letters were sent outside the Royal Mail and the British postal system in America broke down completely.

Benjamin Franklin, ever the patriot, changed his frank from "Free. B. Franklin" to "B. Free. Franklin." This so aggravated the British that in 1773 they fired him from his job as Deputy Postmaster General for engaging in "pernicious activity on behalf of the Colonies." (Philadelphians *like* that story.)

The early days of airmail also provide many anecdotes for postal speeches. At the dedication of the 8-cent airmail stamp in 1962, I talked about the outstanding airmail pilot of all time, Charles Lindbergh, who flew his DeHaviland on Contract Route No. 2 held by the Robertson Aircraft Corporation between Chicago and St. Louis. Flying northbound on this route in 1926, Lindergh ran out of fuel and was forced to jump. Dean Smith, a colleague of Lindbergh's in the airmail service, reported a crash landing tersely: "Landed on cow—killed cow—scared me. Smith." Another airmail pilot, Kenneth Unger, crashed in a field after engine failure. Unhurt, he borrowed a horse to return to town, but he handled the horse less skillfully. The horse threw him for another crash landing and that time he broke his ankle.

The very first load of airmail was sent out from Washington to Philadelphia on the morning of May 15, 1918. A distinguished group including President Wilson and Franklin D. Roosevelt, then a young Assistant Secretary of the Navy, saw the pilot off. But his directional signals got a little mixed up, and the pioneer airmail sack wound up in Waldorf, Maryland, instead of Philadelphia. The mail had to be carried back to Washington by train.

On one occasion President Kennedy and several cabinet and other top officials addressed a foreign trade meeting in the rather dully illuminated Mayflower Hotel ballroom. Listeners and speakers were distracted by a persistent clatter from a metal stairway to the balcony. If they could have investigated, they would have found a little man struggling clumsily to carry a huge spotlight mounted on a tripod to the top of the stairs. For every two steps up he fell back one with resulting din resounding amid the speeches. Finally, in the long speaking program a rather stuck-on-himself undersecretary came to the podium. Suddenly, he and he

alone was glaringly spotlighted by the bulky equipment he had
had his aide wrestle upstairs for the purpose.

This same undersecretary at an unofficial White House dinner
once delivered himself of a flowery toast to a guest he mistakenly
thought was Prince Radziwill, Mrs. Kennedy's brother-in-law.
Unhappily, Prince Radziwill was on the other side of the ocean
and the target for the toast was, in fact, Mrs. Kennedy's dress
designer.

When speaking in public, it helps a great deal to master the
quick retort and the ready laugh. Appearing on the same plat-
form with Bobby Kennedy I mentioned that half of our 35,000
postmasters were women. Bobby got up immediately afterward
and said, "It's all right about 50 per cent of postmasters being
women, but I think it is even more important that only 5 per cent
of the inmates of our federal prisons are women." That is the
quick retort.

Hubert Humphrey offers the ready laugh. Referring to his
defeat by Kennedy in the West Virginia primary, Humphrey
said that he hadn't done badly for a Protestant. "It isn't impossible for a little man (meaning himself) to defeat a big man
(Kennedy)," he observed. "After all, David slew Goliath. Of
course, that was sufficiently unusual so that three thousand years
later people are still talking about it." Humphrey made these
remarks shortly after the Cuban missile crisis of 1962. There had
been a sensational *Saturday Evening Post* story in which Charles
Bartlett and Stewart Alsop tried to do a hatchet job on Adlai
Stevenson by unfairly ascribing to him a "soft" approach to the
Cuban problem. "We've all been busy reading Bartlett's Quota-
tions and Alsop's Fables," said Hubert.

In a speech before the Alfalfa Club in Washingon in early
1961, President Kennedy poked sly fun at a prominent Washington lawyer who makes a point of knowing people in high places
and who reportedly received a fee of 5 million dollars following
passage of an important piece of business legislation. Said Kennedy: "This man is a modest, self-effacing, unselfish, dedicated
citizen. All he asks in exchange for his selfless assistance to office
holders is—to have the name of his law firm printed on every
dollar bill!"

Politics and religion, it is said, with more than a grain of wisdom, are two topics to avoid, unless you're looking for an argument. But in Washington, where everybody loves an argument anyway and most things are topsy-turvy, politics can't be avoided and religion isn't. The two are a most fruitful source of anecdotes for after-dinner speakers.

At the dedication of Cardinal Spellman's philatelic museum in Weston, Massachusetts, the Cardinal asked me to join him in planting a dedicatory tree. I demurred. "Don't you remember what happened to President Kennedy's back when he planted a tree in Ottawa?" I asked.

"Here, take this shovel," said the Cardinal. "While you're digging, I'll rub your back and pray for you." And he did.

Cardinal Spellman is one of the top stamp collectors in the world. Years ago his invaluable collection was stolen from his residence and has never been recovered. But he has now built up another notable collection.

When I took office I found that my predecessor had for years been sending a special, official presentation album of each new U.S. stamp issue to Cardinal Spellman, a favor not accorded to any other non-government figure. I felt this was not a good practice to continue in the administration of a Catholic President. I asked President Kennedy about it and he agreed with me, so I stopped sending the albums. Before long I began receiving urgent pleas from "Big Jim" Farley to resume sending the special leather folders of stamps to his good friend the Cardinal. I solved the problem by telling Jim I would send *him* each new album in his capacity as a former Postmaster General, indicating that what he did with the albums after he received them was no concern of mine. As a result the Cardinal has a full set.

George Romney, Michigan's Mormon Governor, was speaking to the Gridiron Club shortly after his election. Addressing himself to President Kennedy who sat beside him and referring to the numerous Kennedys in government positions, Romney declared that it would be utterly impossible for him to be President. Each of his Mormon grandfathers had had four wives and therefore he had 231 first cousins. "I could never find jobs in Washington for all of them," he said.

In that same speech the Governor described the opposition in the Senate many decades ago to the seating of Utah's Senator Reed Smoot, a Mormon. Romney quoted Smoot as saying, "I would rather be for a polyg who monogs than for a monog who polygs."

One help to my speech efforts all across the country was that I could claim to be "local" in sixteen different states.

I grew up in Illinois, went to the seventh grade in Miami, Florida, attended law school in Massachusetts, spent my honeymoon in Vermont, lived in Virginia the first year of World War II, spent twelve summer vacations in Michigan, lived in New Jersey four years, New York one summer, California four years, and, after coming to Washington as Postmaster General, resided in Maryland. In addition, as an amateur geneologist I knew that my original American ancestors came from Pennsylvania and Delaware, and migrated first to West Virginia and then to Tennessee. My grandfather Day was born in Arkansas and grew up in Missouri.

An associate of mine in the Post Office Department became mildly annoyed with the regular additions to the list of places of which I was a native son. One morning when the two of us were waiting to pay a call on the powerful Senator Styles Bridges of New Hampshire, my associate said: "I challenge you to get 'local' in his state."

I had never met the Senator before, but when I entered his office I told him that my daughter, Molly, went to camp in the summer at Lisbon, New Hampshire. He immediately began chatting cheerfully about that area as though I were his most authentic constituent. My colleague didn't try me out on any more states.

Calling on members of Congress may not be the practice of all cabinet members but I recommend it highly. When I arrived in Washington in early January, 1961, and even before I was sworn in, I visited a number of key members of the House and Senate Post Office Committees. One was the senior Republican on the House Committee. As we sat visiting in his office, he emphasized his pleasure at my call by saying that in eight years my Republican predecessor had never been in his office.

Nearly every week after I took office, Senator Karl Mundt of South Dakota sent me a carping, cutting letter on some subject or other. I went over to see him. He is quite a Lincoln scholar. We talked about Lincoln and he escorted me to the door with his arm around my shoulder. There were no more insulting letters.

My favorite comment on my speechmaking efforts came from the official newspaper of the Republican National Committee when I resigned. It said the Republicans were glad to see me ending my rounds on the speech circuit since I went over too well with audiences.

A Democrat never received kinder words from the Grand Old Party.

Preparing and delivering speeches is one of the most important parts of the job for any high public official. It forces him to put his ideas together in an orderly, understandable way. It makes him clarify his policies and helps the public to know what his department is trying to do.

It is too bad we have progressed so little in the art of speechmaking. The offerings, for example, at national political conventions seem more dreary and uninspired each four years. Television has done much to make nearly every speech seem trite and to make nearly every speaker seem unnatural and stereotyped.

I am sure political campaigns are much too long and much too expensive. I would like to see us adopt the English system of a three-week limit on campaigning and a low limit on the amount that can be spent by any candidates. In the early days of our country presidential candidates merely made themselves available and did not dash madly about the country risking their lives in a search for votes. Even more recently we have had some "front porch campaigns." There were statements of positions and answers to charges, but less arm pumping and motorcading and general hoopla. I would like to see that approach tried again.

The 1960 Presidential campaign in California was much different from what I had been used to in Illinois and New Jersey. California, under the high-principled leadership of Governor Hiram Johnson nearly fifty years ago, got rid of party machines by eliminating patronage, the abomination which makes machine politics thrive. Whereas in Illinois and Pennsylvania the winning party organization can ladle out tens of thousands of state jobs, in California, the largest state, less than one hundred state jobs are not insulated from politics by civil service. The same is true in county and city jobs there.

As a result, in California there is no all-powerful political boss to crack the whip. The nearest thing to a Democratic boss, Assemblyman Jesse Unruh, was put on the Kennedy organization payroll, but so strong is the anti-boss feeling in California that this caused an unfavorable reaction. The party "doorbell ringers" in California are not public payrollers, but volunteers, organized into hundreds of neighborhood Democratic clubs, and are concerned with issues and ideas rather than party victories. These club adherents are often of the super-liberal stripe with a touch of the "peace at any price" philosophy on international issues.

The club people preferred Adlai Stevenson in 1960. Stevenson told me in February, 1960, that he was not going to be a candidate. Though I was devoted to him, I was sure a "reluctant" candidacy would not work again with such strong contenders in the field as Kennedy and Johnson. So I began plugging for Kennedy long before the national convention.

Even after the nomination the hearts of many of the club people still belonged to Stevenson. The moderate, business-professional Democrats such as myself were all for Kennedy, but there weren't nearly as many of us around the Los Angeles area as there were in Northern California, which is more conservative. In the central valley of California there was a big "Bible belt," anti-Catholic population.

My daughter, Jerry, worked in the Citizens for Kennedy headquarters, but all the time I could take for the campaign had to be devoted to the hard-fought, one-and-three-quarter-billion-dollar water bond referendum, for which I was a principal strategist and fund raiser. One of the few contacts I had with the Presidential campaign was at a gathering of the faithful at the Chapman Park Hotel to hear Robert Kennedy. It was a sparsely attended meeting and Mr. Kennedy was bound to notice that night, as on other California occasions, the sharp contrast with Massachusetts politics. In the golden state, with its absence of patronage, there were no political troops who could be ordered into battle. Later, John Kennedy narrowly lost California.

But, by virtue of having made an objective choice among the Democratic Presidential hopefuls, I happened later, at the 1960 convention, to meet that test which was so all-important to the Kennedys: that of having been "with us before Los Angeles." My agreement to serve as a Kennedy delegate at the convention involved some difficulties. When I asked Prudential if I could accept, the answer at first was "No," that I mustn't be too political. Then there was a change of heart by the wise men at the top of the financial Rock of Gibraltar.

Although Prudential was not as politically benighted as many big business corporations, I am sure that if I had asked permission to be a delegate to the *Republican* convention I would have received not only a prompt "yes," but an approving pat on the back.

Chapter 13
ORIENTATION COURSE
FOR INNOCENTS

THERE is an apocryphal anecdote current in Washington which, if it lacks the substance of fact, has about it the ring of reality. In the story, Sargent Shriver is coaching new Peace Corps recruits: "You will have rocks thrown at you. You will be cursed, insulted, spat upon. Your motives will be questioned. You will be called names. But then, when you leave Washington . . ."

Truly, it takes endurance to be an official in the Government; a certain imperviousness to insult, a lot of stamina and persistence. The Government—that massive bureaucratic entity whose General Services Administration is where its heart ought to be—grants tacit recognition to this state of affairs by displaying a singular lack of confidence in its ability to hold onto its officials. For example, Cabinet officers cannot obtain calling cards with name and title at Government expense. But if the officer is willing to skip the name and settle for title alone (presumably so that his cards can be passed on to the next guy), the Government happily picks up the tab. This is certainly a realistic approach. In Truman's eight years as President he had 34 Cabinet members. At least 3 individuals held each post.

One can readily see that life in Washington is full of pitfalls for the unwary and the uninitiated. I have long felt that there should be a sort of Orientation Course for Innocents, a seminar for newcomers to high office—schooling them in what to avoid in official life—to make their stay more pleasant and their tenure more certain. Subjects covered would include such potential perils as use of limousines and official letterheads, policy on gifts, and problems of expense accounts. Such a school is particularly needed because rules are constantly being changed by whichever paragon is at the moment the acknowledged interpreter of ethical principles. Can a Cabinet member accept an honorarium for making a speech? Good students will know that historically there have been three correct answers to this question: Yes, No, and Maybe. In the Eisenhower Administration the answer was yes. In the Kennedy Administration, by a directive issued in the President's name, it was no, though I don't recall President Kennedy ever talking to the Cabinet about conflict of interest rules. I doubt if the problem was very real or meaningful to him. He gave 100 per cent of his Presidential salary to charity. How could he be expected to concern himself with whether a federal official could or could not accept a 300-dollar honorarium for making a commencement address? How about our distinguished Solons? Do the same rules apply to them? The first thing a Federal appointee must realize is that such rules are not made for Congressmen, who play a role similar to that of the loving but authoritarian father who says, "Do as I say, not as I do."

A Senator can and does charge as much as 1,500 dollars for a speech and 2,500 dollars for a magazine article, but all an official of the Executive Branch can safely accept is a plaque, which probably makes him overweight on his baggage. Should he accept anything more, some Congressman will be sure to rant and rave about it, perhaps even writing about it and other ethical matters, if the pay is good enough.

Like Caesar's wife, the man appointed to high Federal position is expected to be above reproach. "Remember Sherman Adams!" might well be the motto of every official, when it comes to accepting gifts. I have always thought Eisenhower's assistant was castigated far out of proportion to his indiscretions. He proved that pride goes before a fall, but did he have to be brought down with such a murderous thud?

Some of the actions held against officials of the executive branch in major press and Congressional attacks occasionally could result from ignorance or naïveté. This is at least a charitable possibility, however seldom acknowledged. Unless one has followed the pattern of character assassination in Washington, one might not realize that using an official letterhead for a communication on a personal business matter could be parlayed into a horrendous misdeed. And, of course, well-meaning and honorable people quite commonly try to press gifts on public officials or to pick up their bills for hotel and restaurant charges. The likelihood of backlash from such an event is remote. But every so often a Goldfine turns up, followed by a Sherman Adams turned out of office.

What the rules on gifts really are or should be is an unresolved question. Obviously a public official can allow someone to give him a cigar. Just as obviously he can't accept a deep freeze, or a mink (or vicuña) coat. But what about a *box* of cigars? When I received a box shortly after taking office, I gave it to a newspaper man who came in to see me. He considered my attitude a great joke. Senator Paul Douglas draws the line on acceptable gifts at $2.50 face value. My own standard is a little different: if it's something you'd like to have, such as a watch or a pair of cufflinks, don't take it from any source with which you will have even a remote official relationship. If it's something you don't want at all—a plaque, a key to a city, a paperweight—go ahead and take it. There was no official Administration policy on such details, but this rule worked very well.

After I had dedicated a post office in Virginia, a hospitable Chamber of Commerce official sent me a Smithfield ham. Recalling that just such a ham had caused a furor in the Truman era, I quickly disposed of the offending viand, thrusting it on a none too affluent messenger in the office. Then, careful not to have anything that smacked of illicit dealings on the record, I wrote to the Chamber of Commerce man and thanked him for his "hospitality and generosity." Vague enough, I thought, for prying eyes, but specific enough so that my benefactor would feel requited. Instead, he felt put out. His expostulation, "But you didn't thank me for that *ham*," came by return mail.

I had no idea what to do when a Middle Eastern postal chief gave me a handsome album of his country's stamps. But not long afterward I was talking to a man working on the Administration's conflict-of-interest rules. I brought out the album to ask him about it. Unknown to me he was an avid stamp collector and, when he saw the album, his eyes lit up. You can guess who has it now!

Gifts from foreign governments to American officials are supposed to be turned over to the State Department to be kept in storage until the official leaves office. On one occasion an official returning from Africa handed over the pelt of a wild animal. Both he and the custodian of the place neglected to note whether the pelt had been tanned. It had not, as was oppressively apparent a few weeks later, when a frantic search began for the source of an indescribable but pungent odor.

Another problem that confronts higher officials is the rule on government automobiles. Cabinet members and a few others are permitted to have their government limousines pick them up at their homes in the morning and deliver them back at night. Others a bit down the chain of command cannot. When the brilliant and hard-working David Bell first became Director of the Budget, he took the bus to his office. When he arrived there a chauffeured limousine awaited his full-time use. Knowing how hard-pressed he was for time and how overworked, I told him he was foolish not to ride to and from his office in the government car, since it would give him a chance to do some of his official reading en route.

Should a Cabinet officer's wife ride to the grocery store in his government limousine? My wife and I didn't think so, but my predecessor told me that it was always done and that my wife should feel free to do it. (She didn't.)

It is difficult for the unwary to appreciate that a man in public office must avoid not merely what *is* wrong, but what his detractors and hecklers can twist around to *seem* wrong. Years ago an elected official in a Middle Western state—a decent, warm man and a good friend of mine—found that his long-time secretary had become too difficult to deal with and he let her go. She had been preparing for this event by secretly retaining a copy of each of the man's expense vouchers. She released these after leaving his employ, with detailed charges as to their impropriety. Her vindictiveness resulted in endless bad publicity for this official. (Of course, an attack in the press does not necessarily mean ruin.)

We hear a good deal about the political power of the press— and it is immense, heaven knows—but public opinion cannot always be swayed. For example, the Chicago *Tribune* has for years been the most widely read newspaper in the Chicago area. It is also about as super-Republican as it could be, and its competitors are not exactly supporters of the Democratic Party. But at the end of 1961, forty-six out of fifty Chicago aldermen were Democrats, the mayor and all the elected city officials were Democrats, and all the elected state officials in Illinois, with one exception, were Democrats. (Maybe the Democrats need more Chicago *Tribunes*.)

In the capital of the Western world, press and partisans hover ready to pounce at the merest hint of error. Merciless on the scent of sin, they rip and tear their prey for very slight cause, giving no quarter. This is well illustrated by the case of Ros Gilpatric, a case which lends credibility and poignancy to the Sargent Shriver anecdote at the beginning of this chapter. Gilpatric left a large New York law firm to come to Washington in the enormously difficult job of Deputy Secretary of Defense. He said at the outset that he could stay only two and a half years and, in the winter of 1962–1963, he announced that he would resign on July 1, as he had planned. In May and June there were a great many goodbye parties for the Gilpatrics.

In the meantime the storm over the TFX fighter-bomber contract blew up. The contract was potentially worth six billion dollars. It was awarded to General Dynamics, but some thought it should have gone to Boeing. The battle raged hot and heavy before Senator McClellan's committee. As a key witness, Gilpatric was warned that he must defend his choice of General Dynamics. The investigating committee called this one and that one to testify, but not Gilpatric, who was left to cool his heels in the midsummer heat. July first passed, and the rest of the month, and all of the summer and the fall, too, before Gilpatric was finally called to the stand. Then, to add insult to injury, a Republican Congressman burst into print on November first charging Gilpatric with conflict of interest and then *demanding* that he resign.

Gilpatric's case is a real incentive to quit while you're ahead.

Granted all this, why would anyone want to take a position with the Government, especially if it means, as it often does, giving up a prestigious, well-paying civilian job? I have been in and out of government twice, once in Illinois, once in Washington, and received immeasurable satisfaction from both experiences. Many people ask me why a man is willing to risk the abuse and harassment that can come with high public office. The question of what motivates us to take risks and assume burdens when there are easier alternatives is a difficult one; its answer is complex. Someone once said that aside from food and drink and such physical needs, man has four basic desires: for importance, for new experience, for security, for appreciation. I believe most people who take up positions on the exposed front line of public life do it partly because they want to feel important, but mainly because they seek new experience. (Security has nothing to do with it, and appreciation shouldn't have.) No one wants to be bored, and life in Washington is seldom boring, which explains why—with all the drawbacks—very few men who come to the Capital in important jobs ever want to leave. The presence of former officeholders from administrations clear back to Wilson attests the truth of this statement.

A few persons come to Washington for pure, idealistic reasons, searching for meaning and significance in their working lives. Many more come for the excitement, for the glamor of power and publicity.

The sad ones are those who come expecting to be appreciated. They are in for endless frustration. The press and public insist—despite modest pay scales—that all top government jobs are plums which obviously have been eagerly sought after and are being avidly clung to by the incumbents. As a result, they don't see why anyone should be admired or appreciated for holding the job. "Sacrifice" in government service is a polite bromide, but it is not taken seriously by the rank and file of press and public.

No one should expect gratitude. The Chinese believe that one should avoid saving another person's life because the person rescued will feel the rescuer is thereafter obligated to take care of him. Occasionally in our society, too, a person for whom we have done a special kindness seems to feel we have an obligation to him from that time on. I once suggested that the name of a particular man be added to a list of Department people to be recognized with a meritorious service certificate. He received all kinds of publicity and bubbled with appreciation at the time. But a few weeks later his supervisor called and said the man had told him that since the Department had recognized the high order of his merits he ought to get a substantial raise from his current "ditch digger's wages," as he evaluated them.

The supervisor was distressed and disappointed, but he shouldn't have been so surprised. When I was with Prudential, where plaques and awards are part of the stock in trade, I presented to a successful agent before hundreds of his colleagues at a big company banquet not only a huge gold cup and an engraved certificate, but also a white orchid corsage for his wife. His only response was, "Don't I get a lapel button?"

Keeping in mind these early lessons, such an orientation course should keep newly arrived Government officials out of trouble, but not necessarily off the griddle; away from major disappointments, but not necessarily impervious to sudden shocks. The would-be expert needs additional, more subtle refinements, and even then he can't be assured of complete immunity to outrageous fortune's slings and arrows. But the barbs can be blunted a bit.

Form letters can be dangerous, too. Letters of invitation to a building dedication in California were individually typed to make them look "personalized," but they were all exact copies of the letter sent to me. And I do mean exact. In the body of the letter I received was this phrase: ". . . and we hope you will

bring Mrs. Day." Every other invitation likewise urged the recipient to "bring Mrs. Day." Very bad form, for a form letter.

Before the 1962 Congressional election it was widely predicted
the Democrats would lose quite a few seats. They did lose a few
in various parts of the country, but an eight-seat gain in reappor-
tioned California made the election, on the whole, a Democratic
victory. In Colorado, Congressman Peter *Dominick,* a Republican, was elected to the Senate. In New Jersey, my Democratic
friend *Dominick* Daniels was re-elected to the House. "Dear
Congressman," my note of congratulations began. "It was a great
election, particularly the sweep in California. I was especially
glad to hear about your victory." The note was dictated to a girl
who was not my regular secretary, and, sure enough, it went to
Republican Peter Dominick. He acknowledged it with such
grace and gratitude that I didn't know whether he merely sent
me a routine form letter or was giving me the dead-pan treat-
ment. In any case, it was a singularly effective move.

When you're new to Washington, don't be too impressed by
those who put on a good show. One lobbyist actually convinced
his out-of-town boss that he had an "inside track" by getting the
boss's friends and relatives tickets to the Senate Visitors' Gallery.
The tickets are available for the asking in any Senator's office.

And don't believe all you read. At a convention I attended, the
printed program called for a friend of mine to make a speech at
the morning session. At lunch time, two people congratulated
him on his fine speech. Their flattery missed its mark since his
speech had been postponed until the afternoon session.

Speak up, then listen hard. Some insurance executives thought
that as Insurance Commissioner of Illinois I was rather strict in
making them toe the line. After I had left office and gone with
Prudential, Metropolitan Life's President Leroy Lincoln introduced me to some insurance executives in a poorly lighted restaurant at the Edgewater Beach Hotel in Chicago. Leroy did say
former Insurance Commissioner of Illinois, but apparently the
vital modifier was lost in the hubbub because an Aetna executive
turned to me and said, "Whatever happened to that bird who

was your predecessor who went with the Prudential?" If that bird hadn't squawked, he might have heard an enlightening earful.

Do get the name and get it right. Don't be like the American who appeared before a Senate committee a few years ago seeking confirmation as Ambassador to Ceylon. He had to admit that he didn't even know the name of the Prime Minister there.

Learn how to get along with Mother Bell. Let it be said, the telephone can be a tyrant. In this electronically advanced stage of civilization, where the telephone's been ringing for ninety years, secretaries and switchboard operators still go into a tizzy over any and every long-distance call as though it were the first one coming through from outer space. There's no reason why a long-distance caller should be allowed to interrupt a meeting with a man who's taken the trouble to visit you in person. Most urgent telephone messages can just as easily be transmitted by capsule version through your secretary. And if you're the one who's calling, don't assume when you do get through that your party has been sitting there eating bonbons and idly reading movie magazines. Phonevision will at least offer the advantage of showing how busy the other fellow is, too.

If you have a real pest on the telephone and can't break off the conversation, never hang up while he is talking. He'd be insulted, of course. However, you can safely hang up while *you* are talking; he'll think you were accidentally cut off because obviously no one would want to hang up on his own voice.

No one who asks you to make a speech or attend a gathering will take it with good grace if you honestly say you are too busy, too tired, or must spend more time with your family. The only acceptable answer is, "Sorry, I have a previous commitment." And that requires careful record-keeping so that he doesn't find out that you later accepted another invitation. Don't be like the lady who said, "Sorry, I have a subsequent engagement."

Remember, too, that an officeholder can tell a person no twenty times, but if he changes his answer to yes, that person will never complain. Similarly, an officeholder who gets a job for me or one of my relatives is a fine old family friend. But if he gets a job for a relative of someone I don't know, he's a political hack.

One day the "hot line" direct-wire telephone from the White House buzzed at my desk. A Presidential assistant advised that while the President had been dictating some letters to a stenographer, she had taken up with him the problem of her brother who wanted to be a letter carrier but was having difficulty with the civil service requirements. The President wanted the matter looked into. The difficulty turned out not to be serious and I soon had it cleared up. But I couldn't help wondering about the attitude of people who expect the President of the United States, with all his crushing responsibilities, to take time to perform chores suitable for a precinct captain.

Don't become bogged down with time wasters out of a desire to be kind. Even Eleanor Roosevelt in one of her books mentioned the absolute necessity of keeping out low priority or no priority callers. But business can be transacted more easily with people you have gotten to know on a first-name basis, so don't avoid social gatherings. People will insult a stranger in a letter, but seldom an acquaintance to his face.

Another rule for the officeholder, which is hard to adjust to because the public simply refuses to understand there must be such a rule, is that the top man must stoically take the heat for mistakes of judgment committed by his staff. The press at times likes to act as though it thought every decision on every detail was in fact made by the man in charge himself. But delegation, which all the experts admit is the only way to rescue a big organization from chaos and its leader from ulcers, must, in order to work, mean that subordinates are given leeway not just to make decisions but also to make occasional well-meant mistakes. It is all well and good to pretend that every staff error should bring an "off with his head" reaction. There just aren't that many good heads around. After the New York *Herald Tribune* failed to feature Democratic charges about "stock-piling" of strategic materials during the Eisenhower days, the press announced that President Kennedy had canceled the White House subscription. He told me not long afterward that he never knew the subscription had been canceled (by one of his staff) until he read it in the paper, but, although he wished the cancellation hadn't happened, he had to stand back of it.

Another useful rule: don't act too fast on non-urgent or routine matters. Many of them will solve themselves while lying in the in-basket.

Public life would be no fun without a few fights. One becomes known for his enemies as well as his friends. But don't fight on too many fronts at once.

Primed with these precepts, an innocent federal appointee should be able to make his way through Washington, side-stepping scandals, shrugging off vicuña coats, and keeping his feet, not his seat, on the ground. He may even enjoy it.

Chapter 14
THE PROSPERITY
PRESIDENT

MY LAST MEETING with President Kennedy took place on June 14, 1963, when I told him I had to resign for urgent financial reasons. (Jim Farley has told me he went 100,000 dollars into debt during the years he was Postmaster General. The salary was higher then, in real dollars, and income taxes were much, much lower. Personally, as well as governmentally, I don't like living on borrowed money.) The President and I were alone in his office and we talked about many things, including the problems he faced. I told him I thought many of them, such as technological unemployment, really had no short term, sure-fire answer.

Six weeks passed after that talk in his office before I could get him to accept my resignation. Finally I got my good friend, the late Senator Clair Engle of California, to intercede on my behalf. The President accepted my resignation effective August 9, and sent me a letter glowing with praise and appreciation.

After I left, nearly two months passed before a new Postmaster General was sworn in. A short time later the President was tragically dead. And a few months after that an extraordinary enterprise in recording history was under way. Dozens of writers and historians began interviewing hundreds of national and international figures about John Fitzgerald Kennedy; recordings of the interviews would be deposited in the Kennedy Memorial Library at Harvard University. The measure of that intense, terribly alive young man who served as President for two years and ten months was already being taken.

Great efforts are being made to make these interviews frank and objective; eulogies and accolades are not being sought. Those interviewed include not only associates and admirers of the late President, but some who were critics and antagonists—Richard M. Nixon and Roger Blough, board chairman of United States Steel, for example. A handful of those asked to participate in this unique project have been reluctant to give taped interviews on the ground that there has not been enough time to see the Kennedy Presidency in perspective. The problem is one we all must face, but few can resist a prediction. I suspect that future historians will reach two major conclusions about that brief time.

First, I believe that historians will conclude Kennedy was challenging the country to change when the country in fact wanted "normalcy," to borrow the word an undistinguished President, Warren G. Harding, used to describe his Administration. The people of America liked Kennedy's grace and style, but they had vague longings for a more placid and comfortable period than he promised. As a result—it has been said, and quite accurately, a thousand times—Kennedy was more popular than his programs.

Every few days he sent a message to Capitol Hill urging some major piece of legislation, but most of these gathered dust. Advisers urged the President to take his case to the people by barnstorming the country or with "fireside chats" in the manner of FDR. But the fact was, while the people were glad to see and hear Kennedy, and to cheer him frenziedly, they were not in a mood to be stirred up or otherwise challenged. They were not about to shower a recalcitrant Congress with mail and telegrams demanding passage of the President's programs.

By mid-1963 the deadlock between Congress and the White House was so unyielding that a real constitutional crisis existed. Few realize how incredibly bad the situation became. Congress was not merely balking at the President's proposals for new action; it was refusing to pass the appropriations bills to pay for running the executive departments.

All kinds of explanations are offered. Some say that Southern Democrats in Congress were conducting a sit-down strike to protest the personal identification of the Kennedys with the civil rights struggle.

Some say the White House failed to build up steam behind its legislative proposals because of its willingness to compromise too easily and too soon on such vital bills as foreign aid and tax reform.

Some say that Kennedy sent over so many "must" bills that he diluted the urgency of the vital ones. There is nothing in the Constitution to indicate that the success of a President should be measured by the number of his bills that Congress passes. In practice, however, the President has become so involved in the legislative process that he runs for re-election largely on the basis of bills he has gotten enacted or intends to promote. Legislative action becomes confused with executive decision in the voter's mind, and in the President's, too, I fear.

Some say that the whole explanation lies in the loss of Lyndon Johnson and Sam Rayburn as the Democratic generalissimos on Capitol Hill.

All of these factors influenced the situation, but the basic one was that Congress, often labeled a "do-nothing" group, rather accurately reflected the public mood, which was the same as that which prevailed in the 1920's when "the return to normalcy" was under way in the land. Compared to other decades there were so few things for angry young men to be angry about. (For lack of real causes they launched such innane crusades as that against all digital telephone dialing.)

The flaming battle cries of the New Deal era—minimum wages, freedom to bargain collectively, social security, and so on—were old stuff, accepted and functioning. Even the labor unions, once in the vanguard of dynamic liberalism, had become big powers satisfied with their own stake in the status quo. This nostalgia for a placid and comfortable age—despite the John Birchers and their sloganeering solutions, it was not a genuinely conservative movement—frustrated the idealists, the reformers, the crusaders. In their frustration, some liberals said Kennedy lacked enough of a personal commitment to the liberal cause. But the depth of his commitment did not make the difference when in the grass roots there was no ground swell of opinion supporting liberal goals.

Although things were comfortable at home, President Kennedy took office on that January day in 1961 amid a highly revolutionary world situation. As the Secretary of State said in a memorandum presented at the first Cabinet meeting, there was in the world "a turbulence we have not seen since the explosion of Europe into other continents, which began some five centuries ago."

At that same meeting the Eisenhower economic inheritance was summarized by Walter Heller as "seven months of recession, three and a half years of slack, six years of slowdown in growth and two to three years of serious balance-of-payments difficulties." The Secretary of Labor recited statistics on unemployment, then said the problem was worse than the figures showed. Despite the denials of Goldberg's predecessor, the late James Mitchell, the steel strike of 1960 did substantially retard the country's economy. A year after the strike the steel industry was operating at only 45 per cent of capacity and producing less than Russia.

At that meeting Secretary of Commerce Hodges said, in the conduct of the Federal Government the only way the new Administration could go was up. And that brings me to the second major conclusion that historians will make about Kennedy's brief era: he did get the country (i.e., its economic growth rate) moving again. Somehow it happened. The economy started up in 1961 and it's still going strong, despite the fact that *historically* a recession is many months overdue. The prophets of doom scarcely have time to tell us how the government is ruining them because they are so busy counting profits.

It is possible to say that Kennedy had nothing to do with this economic resurgence, that it happened by itself or in spite of him—but it *did* happen, and I think that history may well at least subtitle Kennedy the Prosperity President. By the time of his assassination on November 22, 1963, even some of the most confirmed economic pessimists were beginning to toy with the revolutionary idea that recessions may not be inevitable every two or three years. After all, a dozen years before, businessmen would have scoffed at predictions that the Dow Jones Industrial Average would break 800, that the Gross National Product would exceed 600 billion dollars, or that new automobile sales would hold at record high levels two and three years in a row—all of which happened under Kennedy, and with very little current inflation.

To some it may seem ludicrous to claim that free enterprise took on new vitality during the Kennedy years, when everyone remembers the bitterness of the steel price dispute in May, 1962. But the fact is that it did. Even some of Kennedy's own top economic advisers were predicting a recession for the winter of 1962–1963, but their prophecies never materialized.

President Kennedy grasped one all-important fact: whatever domestic problems our country faces, they are mild compared to what we would be up against if we had a major economic downturn. Five per cent unemployment is a nagging cause for worry, but a real recession could quickly make it an intolerable 10 per cent. A six- or seven-billion-dollar federal deficit causes deep concern, but a major recession could easily triple or quadruple it, just as the 1959 recession turned Eisenhower's predicted half-a-billion-dollar federal surplus into a twelve-and-a-half-billion-dollar deficit. (The unbalanced budget really worried Kennedy.) Even the plaguing problem of Cuba is slightly more bearable when all the world can see our economy rolling in high gear and Castro's economy sick and staggering. President Kennedy was neither "bad" for business nor opposed to it. Indeed, the opposite is true: he was good for business; but he had bad public relations in that sector. After the steel crisis he tried hard to improve his "business image," even requesting biweekly "pro-business" reports from each Cabinet member detailing what had been done for business in the preceding two weeks. The White House used this information to try to combat the anti-business charge.

If a depression had descended while Kennedy was President he would have been blamed for it (just as Hoover was blamed for the depression of the 1930's). But we had unheard-of business prosperity instead. Yet even many Kennedy fans are hesitant to claim he had any connection with it.

The more popular and accepted symbol of the New Frontier is the Peace Corps. The Peace Corps is part of the emphasis on youth, sparkle, and freshness in the Kennedy approach to government and public affairs—an approach heralded by that ringing Presidential utterance, "Ask not what your country can do for you, but what you can do for your country."

President Kennedy will also be remembered for the great skill he employed in projecting his personality and ideas through masterful speeches and highly articulate and self-confident press conferences. These conferences, televised throughout the country, may have contributed more than anything else to the personal identification millions came to feel with John Kennedy—an identification still evident in the sustained high level of public interest in books about him and in assessments of his legacy.

President and Mrs. Kennedy made unprecedented use of the prestige of the White House to emphasize art, beauty, and good taste, fine music and exciting architecture, starting a national craze for culture that reached truly fantastic proportions, with so-called "cultural centers" springing up all over the landscape. In this vein President Kennedy even took a personal interest in the design and appearance of commemorative postage stamps, praising those he felt had style and questioning the unavoidable drab ones. (The artist's conception of a frontier sod house, chosen to commemorate the Homestead Act centennial, was necessarily cheerless; a downright hideous stamp—one of only two I couldn't stop—celebrated the 100th anniversary of basketball.) He told me enthusiastically of the improvement made in the color scheme of his Presidential jet by a well-known consultant in color and design, and urged me to consider using the same man to devise better designs for everything from mailboxes to letter carriers' caps. Such was the extent of the Kennedys' interests that nothing within their range escaped scrutiny, not even the cut of a mailman's cap.

I once observed first-hand the fact that airtight personal security cannot be provided for a President. A year before the assassination, Mrs. Day and I went as guests of Navy Undersecretary and Mrs. Paul Fay in their railroad car on a special Presidential train to the Army-Navy football game in Philadelphia. I believe that is the only train trip President Kennedy took while he was in office and he spent nearly all of it in the Fay's car, where we were, chatting amiably and listening to guitar numbers played by Jim Symington, the Missouri Senator's popular son.

During the first half of the game we in the President's party sat on the Navy side of the stadium. At half time, by tradition, he was to cross the playing field and sit on the Army side. Single columns of cadets and midshipmen marched out and formed an aisle across the field. The President walked halfway across accompanied by four or five military officers and two Secret Service men. Suddenly I noticed a large man in civilian clothes running out from the Army side between the rows of cadets and midshipmen. I am sure each of the latter assumed the man was a reporter or official and had some part in the ceremonies. No one stopped him. The man rushed to within ten feet of the President before a Secret Service man quickly stepped out and blocked his way. Then police ran from the sidelines and dragged him, struggling violently, from the field.

The newspapers quoted him later as saying he only wanted to shake hands with the President. But it was a chilling moment. I worried then—and do now—about such incidents and the safety of our President.

Chapter 15
ALL THE WAY
WITH LBJ

I FIRST LEARNED from my eleven-year-old son, Jimmy, that Lyndon Johnson would stand next in line to the Presidency. Like most of the other delegates to the 1960 Democratic National Convention, I hadn't half as much idea of what was going on there as the people watching it all on television. One afternoon I left my delegate's seat in the Sports Arena and called home. Jimmy answered the phone.

"Pop," he said, "do you know who's going to be the candidate for Vice President?"

"I haven't the slightest idea."

"It's going to be Lyndon Johnson. I just heard him accept on television."

Three years later, John Kennedy was dead, and Lyndon Johnson accepted the responsibilities of the Presidency.

After November, 1963, the legislative stalemate cleared and the constitutional crisis passed. We can speculate as to the reasons for it. There were changes in the role of the White House staff. Johnson began turning out the lights and—not at the same time, of course—dancing with all the Congressmen's wives. But principally I believe that President Johnson is somehow associated in the mind of the public with normalcy and comfortableness in a way that President Kennedy never was. Somehow Johnson gets all sorts of things done, without clarion calls for grass-roots crusades. He tells us things are going pretty well and we are glad to hear it and eager to believe it. He fits well with the prevailing public mood, and with the mood of Congress, which has few crusaders.

I had met Lyndon Johnson only once before he was elected
Vice President—at a jammed reception before a Democratic fund-
raising dinner in Los Angeles. Somehow he knew I was a top
executive of Prudential and held back the aggressive would-be
handshakers while he asked me if Prudential would be willing to
invest in government-guaranteed loans for college dormitories if
such a program became law.

When I went to Washington in early January, 1961, for the
"transition period," I called on the Vice President-elect at his
bustling Capitol office and observed for the first time his ability
simultaneously to converse with a visitor, talk on the telephone,
and read and respond to a blizzard of little typed messages
brought in to him by aides.

I didn't know the top people in the new Administration except
for my slight acquaintance with the President. The only other
Cabinet member I had ever met was Robert Kennedy with
whom I had shaken hands briefly in Los Angeles. The only
member of the new White House staff I could even identify
before December, 1960, was Lawrence O'Brien, who had been in
the candidate's entourage on a couple of the pre-election trips to
California.

At the outset of the Administration, everyone was too busy to
take time out to get acquainted. (Constant self-pitying talk of
long hours, pressure, harassment, telephone calls in the dead of
night, and to and from limousines, has long since become a
stereotyped status symbol among high Washington brass.) But
very early in the game, Mary Louise and I began to feel we knew
the Lyndon Johnsons in a relaxed, pleasant way. I suppose part of
the reason was that we are almost as gregarious as they are.
Parties at their handsome house, "The Elms," which they bought
from Perle Mesta, were genuine fun. After one dinner there, the
Vice President called for silence and had me tell some humorous
stories to the assembled group.

He mingled unassumingly with the Cabinet members at informal luncheon get-togethers we had from time to time at the
various department headquarters (a practice from the Truman
days which I had reinstituted so we could all see more of each

other in between the infrequent formal meetings with the President). On more than one occasion rather early in the Kennedy years, LBJ said there were several of the Cabinet members he hadn't known and wouldn't have appointed but now that he knew them he felt he couldn't have made a better selection to any one of the ten posts.

I hope that someday a thorough and objective resarcher will write the story of LBJ as Vice President. Here was a super dynamo of a man, a "take charge" type, used to power and action, who forced himself into the backseat role which goes with being Vice President, and never slipped up in his performance. He talked at Cabinet meetings but always with careful deference to the chief. He endured with dignity the incredible "inspired" stories of mid-1963 that he might be "dumped" as the Vice-Presidential nominee in 1964.

The reason this story would be of long-term interest is because there is so much built-in frustration in the Vice President's job. Arthur Schlesinger, Jr., once told a group of us that Andrew Jackson and Martin Van Buren were the only President-Vice President team in history who continued to be thoroughly enthusiastic about each other during their years in office. I think Truman—with all his good friends in the Senate—would have been completely satisfied as Franklin Roosevelt's Vice President. But he barely had a chance to find out.

The only place within my sphere where LBJ absolutely refused to play "after you Gaston" on power and prerogatives was on federal patronage in Texas. He said he had had a firm agreement with President Kennedy that he, Johnson, rather than the Democratic Senator, Ralph Yarborough, whom he did not like, would control Texas appointments. There were periodic blowups as the White House wavered on this agreement in the face of furious blasts from Yarborough. Much of this involved postal patronage and I was like a hapless guest at a family brawl. Yarborough demanded I fire a postal official (not civil service) who was from what he considered the enemy faction in the Democratic Party in Texas, and he fought a postal appointment for the brother of

Cliff Carter, one of LBJ's most trusted aides. Brickbats flew every few weeks, but by some miracle my friendship increased with both Yarborough and Johnson.

On a trip to San Antonio the local postmaster, who had been in the job for twenty years or more, described to me in hilarious detail his problems in arranging on short notice the wedding of LBJ and Lady Bird.

A phone call came in the morning from Johnson, who was several hundred miles from San Antonio by car, telling the postmaster to make all arrangements for an eight P.M. wedding that evening at a specified church. When the postmaster tried to say it was impossible, he found LBJ was no longer on the other end of the line and could not be retrieved. The postmaster described to me a day-long obstacle course in persuading the rector to make the church available on such short notice, in obtaining a medical certificate and a marriage license and all the rest. Not knowing Lady Bird's finger size, the postmaster borrowed six different sizes of wedding rings from Sears Roebuck, stuck them through Lady Bird's door when she arrived so she could try them on and keep the right one (later replaced, of course, with a better one), and rushed the other five back to Sears just before the store closed.

As Vice President, LBJ was tireless in performing wearing chores. He flew with me in a helicopter to a national meeting of postal personnel men at a big motel north of Washington. When he had finished his prepared talk—from a podium which, according to his standard instruction, had to be just forty-two inches above the floor—he walked down among the delighted officials and delivered a second ten-minute speech, fervent, hard hitting, and off the cuff. He kept us all moving so fast that a chance photograph taken of our group leaving that meeting made us appear to be doing the twist.

In a remarkable, hour-long extemporaneous speech before the U.S. Chamber of Commerce a few months after he succeeded to office, President Johnson pointed with pride to the fact that we are in "the longest period of uninterrupted prosperity in the

peacetime history of America." Corporate profits—after taxes—
have gone up from 17 billion dollars in 1952 to 27 billion dollars
in 1963 and a predicted 30 billion dollars in 1964, he said, riding
high in the saddle on the economic prosperity left him by John F.
Kennedy, who promised to get the economy moving again, and it
did.

I spent the weekend of the Fourth of July, 1963, at the LBJ
Ranch in Texas. The Vice President phoned me from New York
and asked me to fly to Johnson City with him that night.

After we were airborne, he pulled from his pocket a sheaf of
statistics on federal employment and picked my brains about
them. It was the calm before a classical LBJ tempest-in-a-teapot
storm—a violent but short-lived blowing of the top. Someone has
observed that Johnson does not treat his aides with Emily Post
courtesy. The fact is, though, they realize these flare-ups are only
a by-product of a supercharged constitution, and don't reflect
deep anger or ugliness.

When the personnel statistics were put aside, LBJ asked an
orderly who was serving snacks to bring the new water-skiing
suits. It seemed the Vice President, after an Independence Square
speech in Philadelphia earlier that day, had visited a boat show
where he had purchased several newly perfected foam-rubber
suits which gave water skiers the same buoyancy as life jackets. It
seemed further that the Vice President had intended the suits be
brought along on the plane so they could be tried out by some of
his staff the next day. The problem was that no one seemed to
have told the orderly that the suits existed, let alone that they
were supposed to have been put aboard. When they were not
forthcoming, there was a monumental explosion from the senior
officer present. In between outbursts, there was much scurrying to
send radio messages to locate the missing merchandise. Happily,
the orderly was obviously well-adjusted to weathering such
storms and retained a courteous aplomb through it all.

There was only one couch on the Jetstar plane and, naturally,
when the Vice President offered it to me, I tried to insist he
should occupy it himself. But quite in vain. An overpowering
will soon persuaded me I should stretch out on the couch, al-

though I was never more wide awake. The Vice President whisked off my shoes and covered me with a blanket. For a couple of hours as the various others in the passenger cabin gave themselves to sprawled snoozing, I lay sleepless but with eyes closed and motionless as a mummy.

Suddenly LBJ leaped up and summoned me to the pilot's cabin to get a look at the landing lights of the ranch from the air. We arrived at 3:30 (Washington time) in the morning, talked politics for an hour, had a few brief hours sleep and arose to take the grand tour of his fantastic establishment in a small open car with Johnson at the wheel. After a bit, Johnson headed the car down the bank of the Pedernales River in front of the main house, followed by a Secret Service car. We were not about to ford the stream as I assumed; we just plunged right in "all the way" and went cruising up the river. We were riding, I learned, in a German-built car-boat with propellers I had not noticed when I got in. The Secret Service men, riding in a conventional car, attempted to keep an eye on us, driving up and down the bank as we drove in and out of the river.

In the morning and early afternoon we also (a) inspected and checked out a new "mobile home" guest house; (b) called up various people, including Governor Pat Brown of California, by long-distance telephone; (c) inspected some construction at another one of the ranches; (d) took a ride in a helicopter; (e) cruised on a lake with some of the group water skiing behind and the Vice President and me up on the bow where he talked alternately to me and, by radio-telephone, to the main ranch (to specify the luncheon menu), to other boats, to the postmaster of a nearby town, and to various others; (f) inspected a collection of enormous hogs on the ranch; (g) attended quarter horse races at the county fair at nearby Fredericksburg.

During the drive back with the Vice President from that hot, close, county fair grandstand, with a Secret Service man at the wheel, I had one of the most chilling moments of my life. As we drove along, LBJ suddenly said to the driver: "Quick, turn up the air conditioning. I feel like I can't get any oxygen. I feel just like I did before I had my heart attack."

I remembered to my horror that Lyndon Johnson had had his 1955 heart attack while riding in a car (on his way to a friend's country place in Virginia).

But when the air came on strong, he was soon all right again. It was just an attack of indigestion.

The Vice President had arranged a meeting at the main ranch that afternoon for forty postmasters from all over Texas. I spoke to them for an hour on Post Office problems, answered questions, and then we all piled into cars, car-boat, and helicopter for the forty-mile trip to another of LBJ's six ranches in the area. That was the one with the lake and boats. After a boat ride for all there was a bountiful fish fry. After the postmasters had gone home, six or eight of us (Johnson likes plenty of people around him, just as he likes telephones, and mobility in any form—plane, car, or boat) descended on the cabin of Johnson's eightyish "Cousin Oriole" for the traditional visit with her. While the Vice President lounged on an old iron bed, the rest of the group "explained" to Cousin Oriole that I had made a special trip from Washington to interview her about her recent collision with the car of a rural letter carrier.

Although it was midnight, there was more to come. With flashlights we drove to inspect a small boathouse the Vice President was thinking of renting, crawled through a barbed-wire fence and again checked out the mobile home guest house to see what progress had been made during the day. My host tested the guest house telephone by calling the operators in various nearby towns. Then came a lively and friendly gab fest around the kitchen table with a half-dozen others joining us for some hilarious reminiscing about political doings in Texas.

A recollection that will always stick in my mind was of a devoted and alert colored man of all work who was the recipient of a constant, detailed stream of instructions from LBJ such as: "There's a new ant hill by that oak tree out near the front door. There's some ant poison on the third shelf in the storeroom off the back porch. Put some on it."

Finally the big boss said to his busy retainer, "You'd better get a little notebook and carry it with you so you can remember all these things I'm telling you."

The truest words ever spoken.

The kitchen at the ranch is not only the center of food preparation, it is also the general gathering place, business headquarters, and communications center. Instead of a normal telephone there is a public address outlet and microphone. Messages come in from telephones in houses on the other LBJ ranches, and from planes, cars, and boats. If a voice says, "Come in, Volunteer, this is Number Eight speaking," the cook pushes the skillet of bacon off the fire and answers, "This is Volunteer, come in Number Eight," and so on. It makes for quite a lively breakfast table. Communications are modern, but an early style telephone in Johnson's big ranch office looks as if it could very well have come from the hand of Alexander Graham Bell turned Paul Bunyan. It is three feet high and has a removable receiver the size of an enormous pepper shaker. But it works.

Lyndon Johnson has a warm sense of humor. His wit is not usually thought of as having the style of President Kennedy's, but he is in fact quite capable of bringing off a Kennedy-type witticism. One year my wife and I received back the envelope in which we had sent our Christmas card to the Johnsons. Quite inexplicably and embarrassingly it had been misaddressed to the Johnson's correct street number but to "The Vice President and Mrs. *Kennedy*." The accompanying note from LBJ read, "I'll admit there is quite an invasion. But there's still a Johnson holdout in the Vice Presidency."

More typically, Johnson is an apt and eager teller of stories. Often they have a political point or apply to a political situation in which he finds himself. When Johnson presided at the swearing-in of Joseph W. Barr, a former Representative from Indiana, as a member of the Federal Deposit Insurance Corporation, he regaled a small audience with this yarn:

"In 1958 I was making a speech for a Senator friend of mine, a candidate for the Senate out in Indiana. Just as I went to the podium, a very young, attractive man said to me, 'Don't forget that I'm a candidate for Congress from this district, and mention my name—Joe Barr.'

"So I talked about the glories of the Democratic Party and the necessity of sending a Democrat to the Senate from Indiana.

Then I recalled what this young, attractive fellow had said to me just as I went to the podium, and I said, 'I have one other favor to ask of you. There is a young, progressive, attractive, well-educated fellow who is running for Congress,' and I couldn't think of his name.

" 'I want to tell you people that he is one of the finest candidates I have ever observed,' and I still couldn't think of his name.

"About that time I heard a fellow whisper, 'Barr, Joe Barr.' I looked around and it was the candidate himself. His qualifications impressed me then even more than his name."

Johnson has on many occasions told some of my stories. One which he liked to use for a while has to do with lawyers and judges.

Herman was brought before a tough judge on an assault charge for giving his wife a black eye. When he pleaded for mercy, the judge gave him probation, but the very next day Herman was back for blacking his wife's other eye. The judge was boiling mad. Herman explained, "Well, Judge, it was this way. Yesterday was a difficult day for me—here in court. Judge, my nerves were shot and I thought a little drink might help. It was pretty late when I finally made it home. The little woman was laying for me right in the front hall. The first thing she said was, 'You good-for-nothing drunk!'

"Well, Judge, I thought about my past and I could see that maybe she had a point there. Even when she called me a lazy, no-good bum I could see that maybe she had a point.

"But when she said, 'If that nincompoop of a Judge had had any backbone, you'd be behind bars right now,' that slur on our judiciary was more than I could bear."

When people ask what gives me more satisfaction than anything accomplished during my Post Office tenure, the answer is easy: improved relations between Department top management and the 590,000 employees.

Nearly always in the past there has been a feeling that just any old body could run the Post Office. And so it was a good place to roost the winning party's national chairman.

But being Postmaster General is in fact an incredibly exciting management challenge and the loyal and dedicated employees deserve, not the back of the hand from a politically preoccupied boss, but full-time, imaginative leadership *and*, oh, so important, some *appreciation*.

In scores of post offices large and small where I visited the employees at their work, I was told by forty- and forty-five-year veterans that never before had they ever seen a Postmaster General go on the workroom floor. My visits to work areas at the main Post Office at Baltimore, forty miles from Washington, and Newark, ten miles from Times Square, were as unprecedented as if these establishments had been located in Zanzibar.

When I arrived at post offices the postmaster invariably assumed and wanted to stick to the pattern of the past: some picture taking and hand shaking in his front office, maybe presentation of a key to the city, and then on my way. Instead, at Pittsburgh, I shook at least a thousand hands while weaving my way among the sorting cases. Everywhere I went I sat down with the employee organization leaders and heard what they had to say. I got to know the inside workrooms of the post offices at New York and Washington and Los Angeles as though I worked there.

My constant wish was that we could improve the image of the Post Office; to divorce it from association in the public mind with politics and antiquated bureaucracy and dusty drabness; to make people realize what an amazing organism it is whereby—in contrast to many other countries—you can count on your letter getting there.

Government employees work just as hard or harder than employees in private industry.

For every Bobby Baker there are tens of thousands of straight shooters working for Uncle Sam. And many of those tens of thousands, devoted and dedicated people, work for the wonderful Post Office Department. May each enjoy his appointed round half as much as I did.

Certainly I enjoyed it. I doubt if anyone who ever served in a President's Cabinet enjoyed it as much as I did. I must have gotten a little canceling ink in my blood, because I hated to leave the Post Office. When I resigned, it wound up eleven years of public service for me. I had had the unique honor of serving in